PERGA
of Sci
The 1000-

industrial training and the enjoyment of leisure
Publisher: Robert Maxwell, M.C.

TRANSPORTATION PLANNING, POLICY AND ANALYSIS

THE PERGAMON TEXTBOOK
INSPECTION COPY SERVICE

An inspection copy of any book published in the Pergamon International Library
will gladly be sent to academic staff without obligation for consideration for
course adoption or recommendation. Copies may be retained for a period of 60
days from receipt and returned if not suitable. When a particular title is adopted
or recommended for adoption for class use and the recommendation results in a
sale of 12 or more copies, the inspection copy may be retained with our
compliments. If after examination the lecturer decides that the book is not
suitable for adoption but would like to retain it for his personal library, then a
discount of 10% is allowed on the invoiced price. The Publishers will be pleased to
receive suggestions for revised editions and new titles to be published in this
important International Library.

3

For a complete list of titles and other titles of interest see the end of this book.

Pergamon Urban and Regional Planning Advisory Committee

G. F. CHADWICK, PhD, MA, BScTech, FRTPI, FILA (*Chairman*),
Planning Consultant,
Sometime Professor of Town and Country Planning,
University of Newcastle upon Tyne

D. R. DIAMOND, MA, MSc,
Reader in Regional Planning,
London School of Economics

A. K. F. FALUDI, Dipl-Ing, Dr Techn,
Professor of Planning Theory,
Delft University of Technology

J. K. FRIEND, MA,
Institute for Operational Research

D. C. GILL, BA, FRTPI,
Director of Planning,
Humberside County Council

B. GOODEY, BA, MA,
Senior Lecturer in Urban Analysis and Perception,
Urban Design, Department of Town Planning,
Oxford Polytechnic

D. N. M. STARKIE, BScEcon, MScEcon,
University of Reading
and Government of Western Australia

B. STYLES, BA, MCD, MRPTI,
Divisional Planning Officer,
City of Birmingham Planning Department

TRANSPORTATION PLANNING, POLICY AND ANALYSIS

by

D. N. M. STARKIE

PERGAMON PRESS

OXFORD · NEW YORK · TORONTO
SYDNEY · PARIS · FRANKFURT

U. K.	Pergamon Press Ltd., Headington Hill Hall, Oxford OX3 0BW, England
U. S. A.	Pergamon Press Inc., Maxwell House, Fairview Park, Elmsford, New York 10523, U.S.A.
C A N A D A	Pergamon of Canada Ltd., 75 The East Mall, Toronto, Ontario, Canada
A U S T R A L I A	Pergamon Press (Aust.) Pty. Ltd., 19a Boundary Street, Rushcutters Bay, N.S.W. 2011, Australia
F R A N C E	Pergamon Press SARL, 24 rue des Ecoles, 75240 Paris, Cedex 05, France
W E S T G E R M A N Y	Pergamon Press GmbH, 6242 Kronberg/Taunus, Pferdstrasse 1, Frankfurt-am-Main, West Germany

First edition 1976

Library of Congress Cataloging in Publication Data

Starkie, David Nicholas Martin, 1942-
Transportation planning, policy, and analysis.

(Urban and regional planning series; v. 13) (Pergamon international library of science, technology, engineering and social studies)
Bibliography: p.
Includes index.
1. Transportation planning. 2. Transportation and state. I. Title. II. Series.
HE193.S7 1976   380.5   76-26945
ISBN 0-08-020909-2
ISBN 0-08-020908-4 pbk.

*Typeset by Express Litho Service (Oxford)
and printed in Great Britain by A. Wheaton & Co., Exeter*

Contents

Part One: The 1960's

1 THE EVOLUTION OF MODERN TRANSPORT PLANNING

2 THE ADMINISTRATIVE FRAMEWORK

3 TRAFFIC AND PUBLIC TRANSPORT POLICIES

List of Figures

List of Tables

Preface

The theme in this book follows closely the ideas contained in my *Progress in Planning* series monograph, *Transportation Planning and Public Policy*, published by Pergamon in 1973. The thesis concerns the interrelationship between transport policy and transport planning analysis. The argument is simply that if analytical methods are to play a part in shaping decisions they must address themselves to policy matters and evolve concurrently with policy issues. The keynote should be "will the model proposed faithfully reflect the impact of the policies it is to test"?

This approach has naturally involved reviewing various aspects of transport policy, the main purpose being to identify those trends and general developments that have taken place over the last two decades. With this intention in mind, I have selected policies relating to transport administration, to urban transport, and to the evaluation of different transport proposals. The review is intended to be a synthesis and not a critique.

The synthesis suggests that during the last one or two decades transport policy has altered in a number of fundamental ways. Indeed, what is surprising is the degree to which Government policy, prompted by evolving public attitudes, can change significantly over a comparatively short period of time.

A parallel development was the introduction during the 1960's of new planning methods and techniques. Referred to as Systems Planning, the new approach is closely associated with the use of computers and other facets of modern management science in which mathematics looms large. In relating this new methodology to evolving policies I have tried to avoid using mathematical notation (and the associated jargon). A more exact (and admittedly exacting) approach would have been to relate the comments in the text directly to the mathematical structure of models but instead I have chosen to sacrifice such precision in deference to the narrative. Those interested in mathematical structures are referred to Appendix B and a number of excellent publications mentioned, when appropriate, in the text.

Perth, Western Australia

The 1960's

CHAPTER 1

The Evolution of Modern Transport Planning

THE PLANNING ENVIRONMENT

The process of change in the transport system, as in any system, is a complex one. The speed and level of change will first be determined by the dissatisfaction apparent in current social attitudes. These attitudes are, in fact, formed by previous experience, expectations, and a more informed awareness of alternatives.

The resulting views are conveyed to the political realm, where they are synthesised by the politician as transport problems and, probably after interaction with the technical planning system, result in the formation of broad policy with associated objectives, constraints, and values. These elements emerge from the political process with varying degrees of rigour or exactitude. The objective may, for example, on the one hand be a loosely termed remit to promote public transport, while on the other it may be a more precise intention of carrying a specific proportion of journeys by bus.

The role of the transport-planner is to use his skills to transform such policies into specific proposals. These latter, after further screening and deliberation within the political process, are converted subsequently into changes in the transport system. The alterations might be in the form of investment in new roads, railways, canals, public transport fares, parking charges, changes in traffic regulations, and so on. In various ways such changes will, together with changes in demand resulting from economic growth or social change, modify the performance of the transport system, resulting in a reassessment and a reappraisal of earlier attitudes. Thus, in this elementary form we have a closed cycle of attitude formation, problem definition, formation of objectives, planning, and implementation (see Fig. 1).

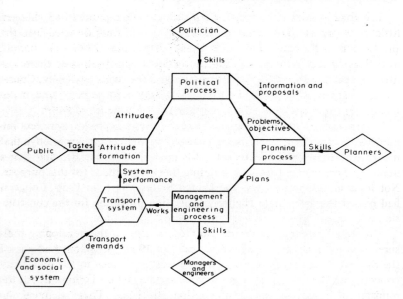

FIG. 1. The planning environment (adapted from Gwilliam, 1974).

Change, however, is not simply confined to the transport system *per se.* At various times pressures develop which eventually lead to adaptions within the planning, political and managerial processes. One way in which pressures arise is from the rapidity with which transport demands have to be assimilated, and it was precisely on account of such factors that, during the late 1950's and early 1960's, the planning component in the paradigm described underwent a fundamental change.

In this particular case the catalyst was provided by economic growth and evolving social values that accompanied growth. Disposable incomes and expenditure on consumer durables grew rapidly and it was the road vehicle, and the car in particular, that both reflected and symbolised this metamorphosis of post-war Britain. Vehicle numbers mushroomed. In the case of the private motor-car the 2·76 million vehicles of 1953 quickly expanded to 5·53 millions just seven years later while the total number of vehicles on the road tripled between 1946 and 1960 (from 3·1 millions to 9·4 millions), a cumulative rate of growth of nearly 8% per annum (see Appendix A).

The road system onto which these vehicles first poured had changed little since pre-war days. During the war resources were diverted into the production of munitions and then, after the 1939—45 period, into flagging export industries and the nation's industrial base: there was little to spare for transport infrastructure and for roads especially. Consequently, expenditure in 1951 on construction, improvement, and maintenance of roads was only £6m more than the 1939 figure of £49m.

In contrast to the post-war road system public attitudes were less immutable. Expectations were being changed by the certain knowledge that it was technically possible to cater for modern motor-traffic and that a number of other countries were building fine motor-roads for this purpose. Not least in this respect was the United States where, in 1956, Congress had passed the Inter-State Highway legislation providing for the construction of a super-highway network to criss-cross the nation.

The initial response of the British Government to the developing pressures was on a rather more modest scale. In 1949 Parliament had passed the Special Roads legislation which gave legal substance to the motorway concept and the first firm proposals were announced by Lennox-Boyd, the Minister of Transport and Civil Aviation, in 1953.[1] These included the Stretford—Eccles, Preston, and Lancaster bypass motorways all of which entered the roads programme. Actual construction was a more hesitant matter and such expenditure as there was for transport infrastructure appeared earmarked for the railways consequent upon the commencement of the railway modernisation plans in 1955.

For roads the turning-point came with the 1957 Parliamentary statement by Watkinson announcing substantially increased expenditure on the construction of a comprehensive network of new highways. This was not, of course, the first of such proposals — the 1946 Barnes motor-roads plan was a much earlier example — but what was different was the determination and conviction involved. In contrast to previous occasions, the proposed expenditure was not cut back with the first squeeze on public investment.

The post-1957 construction programme concentrated upon inter-urban roads, and five specific projects of this nature forming the basis of the modern motorway network were included in Watkinson's statement. This

[1] An historical account of the motorway concept in Britain will be found in Drake *et al.* (1969).

emphasis stemmed from the fact that inter-urban roads were more cost-effective politically and possibly in economic terms too. They were also administratively easier to undertake in view of the Ministry of Transport's direct responsibility for the trunk-road network, and planning them was a conceptually easier task than deciding upon the most appropriate scale and location for urban highways.

THE MODERN PLANNING PROCESS

The initial concentration on inter-urban roads in the spending programme did have the consequence, however, of buying time to enable the more intractable urban transport problems to be given careful consideration.

The outcome of this consideration was the infusion of North American ideas on the methodology of urban transport planning — ideas which gave rise to fundamental changes in the planning process.

These ideas have since been dubbed with various labels, of which systems planning and analytical planning are the two most common. Indeed, the imported methodology did have features — such as a feedback or cyclic elements and the treatment of its subject-matter as a series of inter-related parts or sub-systems — familiar to the cyberneticians, the OR scientist and other exponents of systems theory. Whether and to what degree this approach in transport planning drew directly upon such theoretical work is difficult to determine.

In the United Kingdom the debt was rather less to theory and rather more to the example of North American enterprise in tackling urban transport problems during the 1950's. Faced with the prospect of more money available for urban transport this expertise was called upon in the early 1960's and North American consultants such as Wilbur Smith, Tibbets Abbett/McCarthy & Stratton, and the Traffic Research Corporation were engaged to establish the new systems methodology in British transport planning.

There are a number of both theoretical and practical variations on the systems theme, but the basic elements involved have been idealised by Thomson (Expenditure Committee, 1972a, p. 164) in the following manner:

(a) Definition: what problem is the plan intended to solve?

(b) Diagnosis: what are the causes of the problem?

(c) Projection: how will the problem develop in the future if things are allowed to go on as they are?

(d) Constraints: what are the limits of finance, time, legal powers, politics, within which one must plan?

(e) Options: what possible ways are there of tackling the problem and what are their respective pros and cons?

(f) Formulation: what are the main alternative plans, i.e. packages of the available options within the prevailing constraints?

(g) Testing: how would each of the alternative plans work out in practice? How would they differ in their practical results?

(h) Evaluation: which plan gives greatest value in terms of solving the problems defined in (a)?

In reality the process was less refined, less structured, more oriented towards testing alternatives with the aid of computerised models, and matched more closely the process depicted in Fig. 2 which emphasises a degree of interaction with a steering group or committee.

Subsequent to these analytical stages, the results of the analysis and the concomitant proposals were referred back to the political process for appraisal and appropriation of financial and other resources. Before final implementation, proposals were, of course, subjected to the rigours of the statutory planning inquiry system, an aspect of administrative law with roots in the nineteenth century aiming to assist the Minister in arriving at the best possible decision.[2]

At each of these latter stages the initial analysis may have been rejected or modified, possibly leading to a reappraisal of the earlier "designs" and a revision of the modelling process. The overall approach has been equated therefore with a learning process whereby the apparent problem and initial objectives were viewed as tentative and the sequence of steps involved in the determination of a plan replicated as the true nature of the problem was agreed upon and new ideas for its solution evolved (Boyce *et al.*, 1970).

---

[2] An account of the inquiry process and its development will be found in Wraith and Lamb (1971).

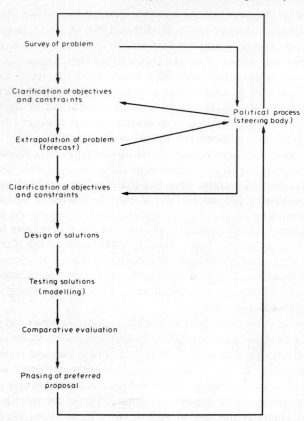

FIG. 2. The transportation planning process.

TRANSPORTATION STUDIES: THE NEW APPROACH

The principal means of implementing this new or systems approach was through long-term transportation studies undertaken during the 1960's in all the conurbations and many of the free-standing towns — towns, that is, with little or no overlap between their transport areas and those of their neighbours.

The first of the major conurbation studies was in London. Its genesis lay in the London Traffic Survey, started in 1961–2, which had the limited objectives of producing traffic forecasts for 1971 and 1981 and related those forecasts to highway networks envisaged for those years.

While this study was still in its early stages, there developed a growing awareness of the significance of transport planning in general urban planning. In 1960 Mr. (now Sir) Colin Buchanan was appointed by the Minister of Transport to study the long-term development of roads and traffic in urban areas and their influences on the urban environment.

The influential, frequently quoted and equally frequently misconstrued Buchanan Report *Traffic in Towns* was published in November 1963. One of its conclusions was that the subject of traffic in towns could be put on a rational quantified basis and this would ease the burden of decision between alternative courses of action. It advocated the preparation of transportation plans for this purpose. In the spirit of this report there followed a joint circular in January 1964 (Circular 1/64) issued by the Ministers of Transport and Local Government. This circular endorsed the main conclusion of the Buchanan Report and stressed the need for local authorities to adopt a co-ordinated approach to land use and transport planning with the aid of transportation studies.

In line with these developments, the Ministry of Transport had decided during 1963 to encourage the launching of such studies in the conurbations by offering to help with their technical direction and to share the cost with the local authorities concerned. As a consequence a transportation study unit was established within the MoT organisation (see page 20) and transportation study expenditure made eligible for specific central government grants at the rate of 50% of costs. In addition, the Ministry was instrumental in bringing together those authorities where participation was essential to the overall success of the study. This was no easy task. Typically, a conurbation transportation study depended upon the co-operation of perhaps two or three County Councils, six or seven County Borough Councils, the major bus operators, and British Railways.

The first of these assisted studies was the West Midlands Transportation Study. Discussion with the local authorities and local transport operators led to the appointment of consultants, and data collection began in September 1964.

Following upon the West Midlands Transportation Study, other conurbation studies were launched as follows: Teesside in July 1965, Greater Manchester (SELNEC)[3] in November 1965, Merseyside in June 1966, and West Yorkshire in April 1967.

During this same period, studies were started in a considerable number of free-standing towns. The largest of these was for Brighton in May 1965, Coventry in April 1967, and Hull and North Staffordshire, both in September 1967. Brief details of these and the conurbation studies are given in Table 1.

Towards the end of the decade there was an increasing tendency for the transportation-study approach to pass both up and down the administrative hierarchy, to deal with movements between urban areas on the one hand and within the smaller urban centres on the other. The urban areas received encouragement from the Ministry of Transport in 1968 with the publication of Roads Circular 1/68, *Traffic and Transport Plans*. This called upon urban authorities in towns of over 50,000 population and all traffic and parking authorities *in* the provincial conurbations (the latter using the conurbation studies as a framework) to send in short-term traffic and transport plans covering the period up to the mid-1970's.

The Circular endorsed an analytical approach and suggested that

broadly [the plan] should state
  (i) the present and future situation (traffic and transport, etc.) as far as possible in quantitative terms;
  (ii) the local authority's transport objectives against the town planning background;
  (iii) the criteria, guidelines and rules of thumb (however crude) which the local authority has applied at arriving at its plan;
  (iv) alternative strategies considered;
  (v) the chosen plan and its cost.

The Circular went on to stress the importance of the systematic and comprehensive consideration of available information, the problems, the objectives, and the means of achieving them. But progress on these urban studies was slow. During the late 1960's few had started, so that by early 1972 only fifty or sixty out of about 140 or 150 authorities had submitted completed plans.

The first truly regional transportation study was possibly the East Central Scotland Study commissioned in 1966, although some conurbation studies, particularly that in West Yorkshire, focused upon movements

[3] SELNEC is the acronym for South-East Lancashire/North-East Cheshire.

TABLE 1. First-generation transportation studies in the
conurbations and larger free-standing towns
(*adapted from Spence, 1968*)

Study area	Population (millions)	Study phase	Organization conducting transport-study phase	Approx. starting date	Approx. completion date
Leicester	0.45	Main	Local authority staff	Jan. '63	Dec. '64
London	8.8	London Traffic Survey	Freeman, Fox, Wilbur Smith	Jan. '62	July '66
		London Transportation Study Phase III	Freeman, Fox, Wilbur Smith	July '66	Nov. '68
West Midlands	2.5	Main	Freeman, Fox, Wilbur Smith	Sept. '64	Dec. '68
Teesside	0.5	Main	Scott & Wilson, Kirkpatrick	July '65	July '68
Greater Manchester (SELNEC)	2.5	Part I: Surveys	W. S. Atkins	Nov. '65	Mar. '67
		Part II: Forecasts	Local authority/ MoT team	Aug. '67	Mar. '71
Merseyside	1.5	Main	Traffic Research Corporation and seconded local authority staff	June '66	Mar. '69
West Yorkshire	2.1	Main	Traffic Research Corporation and seconded local authority staff	Apr. '67	Dec. '68
Brighton	0.3	Main	Team of local authority staff	May '65	Dec. '68
Coventry	0.3	Main	Team of local authority staff	Apr. '67	Oct. '68
Hull	0.35	Main	Freeman, Fox, Wilbur Smith	Sept. '67	Dec. '69
North Staffs.	0.45	Main	Elliott Traffic Automation	Sept. '67	Dec. '69
Glasgow	1.9	Main	Scott & Wilson Kirkpatrick: Tibbets Abbett/ McCarthy Stratton	1964	1968
Belfast	0.5	Main	R. Travers Morgan (NI)	Apr. '65	June '69
Cardiff	0.32	Probe Main	W. S. Atkins	Apr. '65 Apr. '66	Mar. '66 Apr. '68

Note: The dates given are only approximate and the interpretation of what
constitutes a commencing or completion date can differ between studies.

between urban centres. The Scottish study covered 1098 square miles of land surrounding the Forth Basin with a population of 1·2 millions, of which less than half lived in Edinburgh.

Some of the regional and sub-regional land-use planning studies also had important transport-planning components. Most notable of all in this respect was the *Strategic Plan for the South-East* commissioned in 1968 by the Government, the Standing Conference on London and South-east Regional Planning, and the South-east Planning Council. In this connection transport planning consultants were appointed to recommend, *inter alia*, the appropriate way in which transportation systems should be developed in the light of the planning proposals.

Interest also developed in the late 1960's in setting up a national transportation study focusing upon the highway network. Problems of data availability and computer limitations restricted the outcome of these deliberations, although the inter-urban roads plan of 1970 was based on features of the transportation-study method. In this example the mathematical representation (or model) of vehicle flows on the trunk and principal road network divided England into 1400 zones of population.

PROJECT STUDIES AND THE NEW APPROACH

In addition to the "area-wide" transportation studies there were also "project"-oriented studies in the 1960's which drew upon the essence of a systems methodology.

In the early part of the decade the better-defined task of constructing the inter-urban motorway network had channelled initial resources into this field. Meanwhile, the urban transport problem was considered further and the result of this consideration was, as previously noted, the subsequent adoption of the systems approach. But, increasingly as the decade progressed, inter-urban road planning too was influenced by the new methodology and the result was a more systematic approach to the choice of routes and the determination of priorities for a particular motorway proposal.

In other cases the methodology assisted with the choice of most suitable mode for a specified transport task — e.g. linking Heathrow Airport with Central London (Ministry of Transport, 1970a) — and with choosing alternative sites for airports.

In this latter context the most significant single project was undoubtedly the Third London Airport Study. The Commission on the Third London Airport, otherwise known after its chairman, Roskill, took place at the end of the 1960's. Its terms of reference were "to inquire into the timing of the need for a four-runway airport to cater for the growth of traffic at existing airports serving the London area, to consider the various alternative sites and to recommend which site should be selected". The Commission's work lasted for two and a half years from May 1968 to December 1970 and was notable for including the largest systematic transport research task so far undertaken. It was interesting also for its application of a systems approach to this task matching closely the paradigm of Fig. 2. Starting initially with the problem defined by the Commission's terms of reference, a crude selection procedure was developed and 78 possible airport sites were identified. The procedures were then refined and the number of sites was narrowed down until with the end of the analysis a final preferred site was chosen by the Commission. This preference together with the proposals for its phased implementation was reported to the Secretary of State for the Environment.

FEATURES OF SYSTEMS PLANNING

In spite of the comparatively recent establishment of transport planning with an identity separate from urban and regional planning, a point has been made of the contrast between the "new", or systems-based, approach and the traditional approach. Some persons, such as Baroness Sharp, have given the distinction added significance by referring to the previously fragmented approach as highway planning, traffic planning, etc., and by describing only the more recent comprehensive planning of and for all forms of transport, public and private, as transport planning *per se* (Ministry of Transport 1970b para. 9). The distinction between the old and the new planning may be a somewhat artificial one as it relates to what is essentially an evolutionary process of developing planning methods. But the differences seem important enough to justify a firm distinction.

Kirwan (1969) lists six significant differences between the old and the new. These are:

(i) An explicit concern with methodology.

(ii) A distinction between planning at the micro-level (detail design and layout, etc.) and at the strategic level (total networks and systems of roads, airports, harbours, etc.).

(iii) A concern with transport planning as a process rather than with planning output (plans).

(iv) A determination to separate goals, objectives, and criteria from the descriptive and analytical content of transport planning.

(v) The aim of comprehensiveness.

(vi) A concern with formulating and appraising alternative strategies and hypotheses.

The Aim of Comprehensiveness

Some of these points of contrast are more significant than others, some are not totally independent of each other, and some points have yet to be achieved in their entirety. For example, when considering comprehensiveness, Kirwan's fifth point and a feature stressed by Baroness Sharp, others have referred to the practice of modern transport planning as the "land-use transportation study". This is to overlook the point that only recently has transport planning developed an identity separate from urban and regional planning, of which by necessity it forms an intrinsic part. Until two decades ago planning for transport on the scale of the city, certainly on the scale of the region, was part and parcel of the total design. Abercrombie's wartime plans for London and other cities did not imbue transport with any exclusive quality, nor did they apply any techniques or methods specific to that field.

The change has been subtle; paradoxically it has come at a time when the transport implications of urban and regional activities have been understood more fully, and succinctly expressed in the maxim that traffic is a function of land use.

The change has involved separating transport from the other component parts of the urban and regional system and treating the latter as part of the general environment acting upon and shaping the transport system. Transport was thus highlighted; it became distinct and the focus of separate study. It is within this more restricted context that, through willingness to consider all modes and means of movement together, the basic approach could be said to be comprehensive.[4]

---

[4] Although there were doubts on this score. Pedestrian movement and cycling were ignored in studies almost without exception, and yet the statistics available indicate that a high proportion of total movements are of this type.

Explicit Concern with Methodology

The methodological advances which in part constitute the new planning are associated with the use of computers and rigorous mathematical models for forecasting future travel. The purpose of these models, collectively referred to as the travel model, is to predict the use to be made of the various transport facilities that could be developed. Such forecasts are part and parcel of the process of selection and choice. Forecasting how a proposed system will operate or work and comparing these results with various criteria or rules of acceptability is, in effect, to choose. In the new planning, analytical content is seen as a very necessary prerequisite to the process of formulating and appraising alternative strategies and hypotheses.

More fundamentally, it is explicit analysis — quantification — that draws out the distinction between the old and the new. Again the distinction is to a degree artificial. The collection and subsequent analysis of facts and figures has always been part of the process of planning. And, in the late 1950's, prior to what is generally recognised as the new approach, the MoT were encouraging highway authorities in the larger conurbations to adopt the North American practice of counting vehicles and asking drivers where they came from and where they were going to, and to analyse subsequently the results of such volumetric and origin and destination surveys with the aid of the digital computer.[5] But what was new was not the use of such analytical methods but the emphasis placed upon them. Quantification of the argument must not only be done but be seen to be done.

A Concern with Alternative Strategies

But perhaps the most significant feature of the "new" transport planning is a concern with formulating and appraising alternative strategies and proposals. Indeed, we could argue that it is the very essence of systems planning. Without it the other features of a systems approach — the determination to separate the policy issues of goals, objectives, and criteria from the descriptive and analytic content of planning and the concern with planning as a process rather than with planning output in the form of

[5] The first use of computers in connection with traffic planning was in the SELNEC Highway Planning Study of 1961–2, when they were used to assign traffic to the quickest route in the road network.

plans — lose a great deal of their relevance. Without the formulation of alternative there can be no systematic process of choice, little concern with analysis, and nothing truly to evaluate.

In spite of its crucial importance, the notion of explicit alternative strategies is very recent. The standard practice until the last few years has been for the undisputed "best" plan to emerge from the unrecorded deliberations of the transport planners. This practice pervaded the pre-war road plans, plans of Bressey for the London Region and the war-time proposals of Abercrombie and the London County Council, and it is to be seen also in the earlier proposals for a national motorway network. But it is not exclusive to highway planning. National Ports planning in particular seems imbued with this same weakness, as the National Ports Council's 1965 document, *Port Development: An Interim Plan*, exemplifies.

Two factors contributed in particular to this situation. One was a policy of judging the value of schemes in terms of engineering or technical criteria, a policy which persisted until the 1960's. With certain forms of engineering assessment, it is sufficient to look at, for example, the expected volume of traffic on a proposed new road in order to decide whether or not it is necessary. In marked contrast to this approach in terms of "absolutes", properly applied economic criteria, which became the preferred approach, will always involve the comparison of two situations. One of these will often be the result if nothing further is done to the network than to carry out those schemes to which the planners have already committed themselves. But it was not official policy to judge schemes in economic terms until quite recently, and consequently there was no incentive to compare alternatives.

The other factor which possibly contributed to the one-shot design situation was the lack, or even the total absence, of adequate guidance concerning the financial limitations that the planners could expect. With no information on possible budgets during the different periods of time, the tendency was to develop a rather rigid "ultimate" design or plan. But thinking in terms of the ultimate is not really conducive to thinking in terms of making systematic choices between alternatives, for choice is a function of scarcity.

With urban transport planning, this tendency of focusing upon the ultimate solution persisted until well into the last decade, but the first indications of a significant change in policy are to be found in the terms of reference of *The Report of the Committee on London Roads* (Cmd. 812, HMSO, 1959). The Nugent Committee, established by the Minister of Transport in 1957, was required to "consider present proposals for the improvement of the road system in the County of London and to suggest possible programmes of work for the next twenty years, *based on different levels of expenditure*" (present writer's italics).

In practice, the nature of the Committee's work was one of phasing the "ultimate" network contained in the 1951 LCC Development Plan. With this network as a basis, two possible twenty-year programmes, one with £120m expenditure and the other with £200m, were envisaged. Nevertheless, the point is made that the notion of considering alternatives had been introduced and to a large extent this stemmed from the recognition that some constraint existed on the resources available. Until this time, explicit financial constraints had been absent, although they were perhaps implicitly recognised in the "targets" of inter-urban motorway mileage favoured by the politicians and exemplified by Mr. Ernest Marples's target of 1000 miles for England and Wales by the early 1970's. But by the end of the 1960's loose estimation of target mileage had been invalidated by the policy of requiring expenditure programmes and by the need to measure accurately the real value of proposed new roads. In the 1969 Green Paper, *Roads for the Future: a new inter-urban plan*, the Minister of Transport put the point thus: "It is no longer sufficient to plan in terms of so many miles of road since the nation is concerned with effective networks."

In the urban context more effective guidance on expenditure levels was given as the 1960's decade progressed. The Ministry of Transport showed an increased willingness to use rule-of-thumb methods to provide such guidance by breaking down national projections of expenditure, broadly on a population basis with allowances so far as was possible for particular local circumstances.

Such a change of policy did have a fundamental effect upon the basic approach of the transport planner. The SELNEC transport planners, for example, now saw clearly their task ". . . to be the best way of investing a fixed sum of money which is known to be likely to be available by the design year of the study", and that this was in marked "contrast to the approach traditionally adopted in the past when planning studies have frequently specified a system to cater for the predicted 'need' or 'requirements' of their study area and subsequently sought to justify the cost of the recommended system".

Unfortunately for much of the transport planning of the 1960's the discipline provided by such financial or budget constraints came too late and the influence of tradition and the legacy of past studies remained. The SELNEC planners, for example, had inherited a highway plan drawn up as a consequence of a very large origin and destination road survey in 1960. They felt obliged both to test this ultimate highway plan (albeit in rather a broad-brush technical manner) and to use it as a basis for the smaller road networks, to be subjected to more intensive study within the MoT's recommended financial constraint.

CONCLUSIONS

This aspect of the transportation-study investment budget illustrates well the degree to which the analytical approach is influenced by the constraints placed upon it. These constraints, together with objectives and social values, provide the context within which analysis takes place. Consequently, analysis cannot be judged apart from this framework. In essence the political process specifies the transport problems and agrees the objectives and, tacitly, the procedures used for evaluating alternatives. These considerations are unequivocally bound up with the design of solutions and the subsequent analyses of their performance with the aid of models.

Moreover, the overall process is an evolving one. The nature of the problems changes as time passes; objectives, constraints, and evaluation procedures are varied accordingly. The next three chapters examine these evolutionary aspects in the context of the 1960's: Chapter 2 reviews the administrative framework within which transportation planning took place; Chapter 3 considers evolving policies with regard to urban traffic and public transport and the objectives implicit therein; Chapter 4 examines changing policies with respect to evaluation. All three aspects form a contextual setting for the analytical models developed during the 1960's. These models are both synthesised and examined in Chapter 5.

CHAPTER 2

The Administrative Framework

TRANSPORTATION PLANNING AND CENTRAL GOVERNMENT STRUCTURE

Until November 1970 the planning of transport by central government was focused upon the rather introspective-looking Ministry of Transport, the post-First-World-War legacy of Sir Eric Geddes. The MoT had effective control of most facets of transport, the only exception being civil aviation and airport planning, although at various times (during the 1950's, for example) this too had fallen under the MoT's aegis.[1]

From time to time the Ministry had adapted itself to changing circumstances and developments in the field of transport. In particular, the Ministry tried during the 1960's to adapt itself to the new requirements of transport planning with its emphasis on the comprehensive approach. The establishment of a Transportation Study Unit and the rearrangement of its divisional structure, bringing the Unit and two Urban Transport Policy groups within the ambit of one Under-Secretary (see Table 2), illustrates this point.

However, major lines of separation of significance to a comprehensive approach continued within the organisation. There were three basic strands, one taking care of railways, ports, and regulatory matters; a second concerned in general terms with policy; and a third focused upon highways, with each answerable to a different person at Deputy Secretary level (see Table 2). The consequence is illustrated well by the London situation. Here highways were handled independently from matters relating to the planning and provisions of London's other transport facilities. In fact, highways generally, their long-term planning, and the

[1] Sir Gilmour Jenkins (1959) provides an authoritative early history of the Ministry.

TABLE 2. Organisation of the London headquarters of the Ministry of
Transport, mid-1960's (*Ministry of Transport, 1964a*)

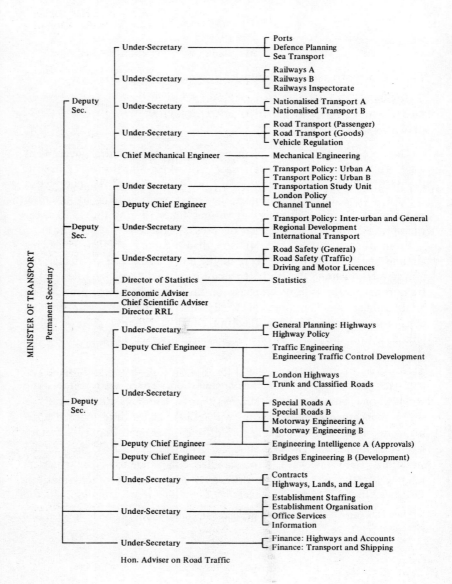

Divisions	Main functions
Ports	All matters relating to ports in Great Britain (excluding railway ports) and to the National Ports Council.
Defence Planning	Defence planning in the transport sphere.
Sea Transport	Sea transport work in connection with the requirements of the Armed Services and other Government departments.
Railways A	General departmental aspects of the activities of British Railways (except passenger closures), including legislation, appointment of Board members, and investment. Railway ports. Light railways and unconventional forms of train.
Railways B	Railways passenger closures.
Railways Inspectorate	Inspection and approval of new railway works, including level crossings; investigation of accidents to trains.
Nationalised Transport A	London Transport Board and Holding Company policy, investment, and general questions; nationalised transport undertakings' pay questions and manufacturing powers.
Nationalised Transport B	General policy for inland waterways; British Waterways Board; pensions, redundancy, and compensation in public sector of transport industry; property questions affecting the nationalised transport undertakings; pipelines.
Road Transport (Passenger)	Road passenger transport public service vehicle licensing.
Road Transport (Goods)	Road goods transport; administrative aspects of scheme for testing of heavier goods vehicles and plating.
Vehicle Regulation	Policy and regulations on construction and use of vehicles and existing vehicle-testing scheme.
Mechanical Engineering	All technical aspects of vehicles including construction, use of, performance, inspection, and testing. Design and maintenance of Ministry-owned plant and equipment, especially for winter maintenance.
Transport Policy: Urban A	Urban transport planning, including implications of Buchanan Report; restraint of traffic; road pricing; "Cars for Cities"; development plans and control of development (except Greater London); advice on and development of traffic management. *(Continued overleaf)*

Divisions	Main functions
Transport Policy: Urban B	Development of policy for and participation in the conduct of land use/transport surveys; urban traffic management and parking policy; road traffic legislation policy; traffic regulation orders (including London).
Transportation Study Unit	Detailed technical planning and supervision of individual land-use transport surveys; assessment and development of techniques.
London Policy	Transport planning for London, including the London Transportation Study, the GLC (Greater London Council) development Plan, major redevelopments, and other matters relating to the planning and provision of London's domestic transport facilities.
Channel Tunnel	The Channel Tunnel project.
Transport Policy: Inter-urban and General	General development of overall transport policy, including economic theory and research.
Regional Development	Transport aspects of the work of Regional Economic Planning.
International Transport	Co-ordination of policy and work in relation to international negotiations and conventions on inland transport issues.
Road Safety (General)	Road safety, including legislation, research campaigns, propaganda, and training.
Road Safety (Traffic)	Administrative aspects of traffic signs, speed limits, and pedestrian crossings; motor rallies.
Driving and Motor Licences	Administration of driving licensing and testing, vehicle licensing, and taxation and insurance.
Statistics	Statistical data, studies, and advice in relation to inland transport.
General Planning: Highways	Long-term planning of highways; size, composition, and control of the road programme; current highway expenditure.
Highway Policy	Review of the highway grant structure; classified and trunk-road general-policy matters.
London Highways	Trunk and classified road scheme and management work within the GLC area. This division also carries out the normal function of a divisional road engineer in respect of the GLC and London boroughs.
Trunk and Classified Roads	Trunk and classified road scheme and management work, outside GLC area, in so far as it is not the

(Continued opposite)

Divisions	Main functions
	delegated responsibility of divisional road engineers; liaison with divisional road engineers.
Traffic Engineering	Engineering aspects of traffic signs, traffic signals, street lighting, pedestrian crossings, traffic orders and regulations.
Engineering Traffic Control Development	General development of equipment associated with traffic signals, pedestrian crossings, and similar control devices; area traffic-control systems; traffic engineering of area traffic-control scheme in West London.
Bridges Engineering	Standards of bridge design, construction and maintenance; approval of bridge proposals; authorisation of movement of abnormal indivisible loads.
Engineering Intelligence	Review of general specifications; development trials on soils and road materials or construction; cost index studies; documentation and classification of technical information; liaison with Road Research Laboratory.
Motorway Engineering A	Motorway studies and engineering scheme work.
Motorway Engineering B	Motorway programme, cost studies, and standard of design; motorway surveys and engineering scheme work.
Special Roads A and B	Administrative aspects of motorway construction and management.
Contracts	Contract letting and claims; agreements with consultants and local authorities.
Establishment Staffing, Establishment Organisation, Office Services	Questions of personnel and accommodation.
Information	The department's press and information service.
Finance: Highways and Accounts	Highways finance; accounting functions for the whole department.
Finance: Transport and Shipping	Finance matters affecting nationalised transport, ports, road transport, Channel Tunnel, and the department's shipping functions.

composition and control of the nation's total road programme remained a separate aspect largely isolated from the broader issues of transport planning.

A further weakness pointed to in such an organisation structure was the comparatively poor relationship struck with land-use planning; the planning process was effectively split between two Ministers.

There were points of contact, of course, between land-use and transport planners, some of which had been presented by legislation prior to the Second World War. In 1935, for example, the Government had awoken to the dangers of ribbon development and its effect on the free movement of road vehicles by passing the Restriction of Ribbon Development Act. The Act's most important provision was that it became unlawful to construct any building within 220 feet from the centre of a classified road without the consent of the highway authority.

The Town and Country Planning Acts provided further contact. The 1947 Act had the effect of requiring local planning authorities to prepare statutory development plans showing the approximate position of future roads for which land needed to be reserved.

But a serious division of responsibilities remained and was brought into the open with the publication of the Buchanan Report *Traffic in Towns* in 1963. The Report concluded that very few statutory development plans really faced up to the problems of traffic and transport (para. 445); it pressed the idea that land use and movement were inextricably linked and it suggested a much closer co-operation between the central and local authority departments involved (para. 479).

The immediate response was the publication of joint circulars and joint planning bulletins by the Ministries of Transport and Housing and Local Government and this was an increasing practice during the 1960's. But the really significant response did not come until the turn of the decade with the formation of the Department of the Environment, concentrating under one Secretary of State all the statutory powers, budgetary control, and political decision-making which had previously belonged to three separate Ministers and Ministries: Transport, Public Building and Works, and Housing and Local Government.

TRANSPORT PLANNING AND LOCAL GOVERNMENT STRUCTURE

Quite apart from the transport-planning agencies of the central government, during the 1960's there were over 800 highway authorities, nearly 400 traffic authorities, and well over 100 parking authorities, all concerned to a degree with the planning of transport at the local level. In addition, local authorities operated 80 municipal public transport services, controlled 44 of the 185 recognised seaports and the greater proportion of the nation's airports. The position was exceedingly complex.

At the time that "modern" transportation planning was first coming into its own the basic distribution of responsibility for highway planning between the Ministry of Transport and the local authorities was established by the Local Government Act of 1929 and the Trunk Roads Act of 1936. Since 1936 the major inter-urban roads have become trunk roads for which formerly the Minister of Transport and now the Department of the Environment have the responsibility. Although the design and supervision of trunk-road works was delegated to the county councils, and then after 1967 to the regional Road Construction units, the prime responsibility for trunk-road planning continued to rest with the central government. Within urban areas, although there were a few "Department roads", the primary responsibility lay in contrast with the county borough councils, the non-county boroughs, the urban district councils, and occasionally the county councils.

Local authorities were under no statutory obligation to control traffic and parking in any particular way. The basis of their responsibilities for traffic was the argument that road traffic and parking space can best be controlled by the local authorities most competent to deal with problems created by local conditions, and for most sizeable towns regulation was therefore entrusted to the town council.

During the 1960's, this structure of responsibility was under great stress and faced criticism for its lack of comprehensiveness. If comprehensive planning was to be a keynote of a modern approach, then the administrative structure of transport planning should reflect this requirement. The need was for local authorities to comprehend in their planning as much as possible of the territory in which interrelated transport movements took place. It was argued that they must possess a jurisdiction wide enough to take into account interrelated factors of town planning, highways, and traffic enforcement. They must be organised so as to cover a wide enough area to cater for the pattern of travel affected by these measures. In the event, the legislative framework existing in the 1960's failed to measure up to these requirements, having been formulated in the very different circumstances of the 1930's. The problem was accentuated firstly by outdated local authority boundaries which failed to reflect the ebb and flow of daily movements, and therefore the complete gains and losses attached to any planning measure, and secondly by a reluctance on the part of authorities to co-operate to overcome these weaknesses. Agreement was particularly difficult in areas where urban development was intense and which were divided and sub-divided administratively into counties, county boroughs, and county districts, even though it was in these very areas that there existed the greatest need for imaginative and timely transport planning. By 1967, for example, in only two conurbations did there exist the formal machinery for co-ordinating local authorities' traffic policies over the whole of the built-up area.

A further problem was the misuse of the scarce manpower resources. By the latter half of the 1960's most local authorities had substantial vacancies for staff to undertake transport-planning work and a worrying turnover of personnel. The report by Lady Sharp, *Transport Planning: the men for the job*, emphasised how wasteful the system of local government as it then existed really was, with productivity varying considerably and often in inverse relationship to the size of the authority.

In those authorities vested with comprehensive control of the various transport functions and planning tasks, chiefly the county boroughs, the Sharp Report found a disquieting proliferation of committees. A survey showed that half the sample authorities had more than one committee dealing with transport matters (quite apart from land-use planning and redevelopment); those running bus fleets were almost always managing them through a separate public transport or trading committee. The general isolation of public transport in the transport-planning organisation of local authorities is something that emerged very clearly. On the wider issue of bringing together transport and land-use planning at committee level the picture was equally if not more discouraging. In only two out of twenty-three county and county borough councils surveyed was this in fact done.

THE ORGANISATION OF CONURBATION TRANSPORTATION STUDIES

The conurbation transportation studies of the 1960's had to improvise to overcome these difficulties. Comprehensiveness in both a geographical and a modal sense was their very *raison d'être* and to achieve this they had to be innovatory in their organisation.

The early studies were organised on the basis of a steering and technical committee (Fig. 3). The steering committee, which met infrequently to provide overall policy direction, was made up from elected members of the local planning and highway authorities together with representatives of the major operators of public transport (both bus and rail) and of the central government. The technical committee, which met more frequently to agree on such matters as planning assumptions and alternative transport systems to be examined, was composed of professional officers

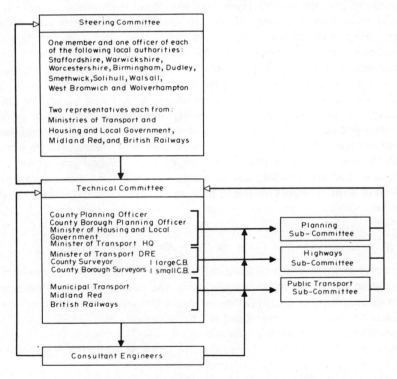

FIG. 3. The West Midlands Transportation Study: the composition of the study organisation (Borg, 1968)

representing those bodies on the steering committee. Working within this framework was the study team, usually staffed by consultants who were in charge of the day-to-day running of the study. In the later studies there were changes in the relative roles of the consultant and the local authorities in the responsibility for the day-to-day work. In the Merseyside and West Yorkshire studies, from the beginning, the consultant only provided a study director and a small number of key personnel, the remainder of the technical staff being seconded from the local authorities and transport operators. The SELNEC Study started in 1965 as the sole responsibility of consultants, but when the data collection phase was completed early in 1967 it became the responsibility of a joint local authority and Ministry of Transport team. Most of the smaller studies in urban areas have been carried out directly by local authority staff with specialist advice as necessary on the computing aspects. In the larger studies the pattern had varied — Hull and North Staffordshire were the responsibility of consultants, while the Brighton and Coventry studies were carried out by specially created teams of local authority staff.

It was intended that the continuation and updating of various studies should be done solely by local authority staff with expert advice from central government and consultants on specialist matters only. One of the first transportation studies to be handed over as it passed into its later phases was the London study. The reorganisation of local government in London and the establishment of the Greater London Council provided the scope and resources for this to be done.

THE ESTABLISHMENT OF THE GREATER LONDON COUNCIL AND PASSENGER TRANSPORT AUTHORITIES

The formation of the GLC was a first step towards making the structure of local government compatible with the requirements of modern transport planning. Incorporating many of the recommendations of the Royal Commission on London Government, the 1963 London Government Act created a system whereby the GLC became the strategic planning authority with responsibility for, amongst other things, preparing a development plan for the metropolis as a whole.

Matching this, the Council became the highway authority for 560 miles of metropolitan roads which had a major traffic-carrying function and, yet more comprehensively, traffic authority for all roads except trunk roads.[2]

Missing from the portfolio was responsibility for public transport, a situation rectified by the Transport (London) Act 1969. Overall responsibility for London Transport was transferred by the Act from the Ministry of Transport, and the Greater London Council was given the task of laying down principles including broad levels of service and financial objectives. In addition, the Council had powers to make both capital and revenue grants not only to the Executive but also to British Railways.[3]

The Act imposed a statutory duty on the Council to produce transport plans and, in keeping with this new status as transport planning authority for London, the GLC was given further highway and traffic responsibilities in addition to overall control of London Transport.

Reform in other major conurbations outside London focused upon the implementation of the 1968 Transport Act proposals for Statutory Passenger Transport Authorities.[4]

Under the 1968 Transport Act, four Passenger Transport Areas were set up, covering Merseyside, the SELNEC area, the West Midlands and Tyneside conurbations, integrating services previously shared between a number of municipal operators. In the Merseyside area, for example, the three municipal undertakings of Liverpool, Birkenhead, and Wallasey were transferred in December of 1969 to the Passenger Transport Authority constituted earlier that year. The PTAs were composed almost wholly of representatives of all the local authorities in the area and were expected to establish policy for a professional executive, which had titular ownership of the undertaking and was responsible for day-to-day management of services.

The Transport Act of 1968 obliged the Authority and Executive "to secure or promote the provision of a properly integrated and efficient system of public transport, to meet the needs of the Area". For this purpose the Authorities and Executives were required to reach agreement with the British Railways Boards and the then newly formed National Bus Company, both of which also provided services in each of the four areas.

[2] A comprehensive account of transport planning in London will be found in Collins and Pharoah (1974).

[3] Rhodes (1972) has argued that the lack of the GLC's executive powers with respect to public transport prior to 1969 led to the impression of highway bias in the Greater London Development Plan proposals.

[4] For a comprehensive account see Hovell *et al.* (1975) and Smith (1974).

Agreement reached with the bus companies enabled PTAs to determine the level of fares and to control the pattern of bus services. With the railways, agreement had to be reached with regard to those services which the Authorities considered should continue and which they were prepared to support financially. It is a measure of the degree to which integration was realised and reflected the geographical realities of daily movement that these agreements enabled the PTAs to control and have influence over facilities provided by public transport within a radius of 25 miles.

In this rather limited way some semblance of co-ordinated public transport policy was possible, although overall parking responsibilities, together with traffic management and highway planning, remained diffused between the many local authorities existing in the PTA's area.

CHAPTER 3

Traffic and Public Transport Policies

ATTEMPTS TO ACCOMMODATE THE CAR

Government policy may have failed to define the *real* choice with respect to the car, as Plowden (1971) has suggested, but it would be wrong to assume that there has not been a better definition of some options. Indeed, notable strides have been made in this respect over the last ten to fifteen years, particularly in relation to urban transportation.

The history of motor-car policy, and therefore that of all road vehicles, for the first fifty or so years of this century was broadly one of *laissez-faire*. There may at times have been signs of a definite policy emerging with respect to the use of vehicles, but, generally speaking, these were but straws in the wind. As long as it was assumed that a ceiling would be reached far short of universal car-ownership there was no need to consider imposing artificial restrictions on the use of the car. Those taxes and other fiscal and monetary controls which were imposed were largely a consequence of an attempt to use motoring as an economic regulator in the context of total consumer demand in the economy.

In 1945 the Ministry of Transport estimated traffic increases by 1965 of 75% over 1933 figures in urban areas and 45% in rural areas. By 1950 — five years later — the number of vehicles had nearly doubled compared with 1933. In 1954 the Ministry told highway authorities to plan for a 75% increase in traffic by 1974. But by 1962 the number of vehicles was already 75% above the 1954 figure. In 1957 the Ministry forecast that there would be 8 million vehicles by 1960, but there were in fact 9 million. In 1959 the Parliamentary Secretary to the Ministry of Transport forecast that there would be 12½ million vehicles by 1969, but this figure was passed before the end of 1964. Given this propensity on the part of the Ministry of Transport to underestimate time and again the situation, it

31

is easy to see why policy remained wedded to the notion that the urban transport problem could be solved by building to accommodate traffic. The attitude in 1950 of the Ministry of Transport's London and Home Counties Traffic Advisory Committee typified in fact the official attitude for much of the rest of that decade — all its proposals were aimed at making it possible for the largest possible number of people to use their cars in Central London. There were to be no restrictions on any type of vehicle, a policy proposal which still found its ardent advocates thirteen years later in the form of the Crowther group steering "the study of the long-term problems of traffic in urban areas", the study named after Buchanan, the chairman of the working group.

Although the finance to build new roads, to expand the capacity of the existing systems, was not forthcoming, planning nevertheless was wedded to the idea of building the problem away — a policy of "more of the same". The slow realisation during the later 1950's that saturation levels of car-ownership were far from reached and the continued reluctance of the Treasury to spend on transport infrastructure led to a change of what one might term tactics rather than strategy. In the mid and late 1950's restriction of the motorist remained politically unacceptable so that attention began to turn, instead, to the notion of increasing the *technical* efficiency of the existing transport system through the application of comprehensive traffic management techniques — what the critics have disarmingly referred to as trying to pour a quart into a pint pot. The appealing aspect of comprehensive management at this time of financial stringency was thought to lie "in the fact that it brings worth-while gains in return for a relatively small outlay of money". In 1960 the Ministry set up the London Traffic Management Unit to try to encourage the spread of traffic-management techniques, and this was supplemented in 1965 by the Traffic Advisory Unit in order to extend throughout the country the expertise gained in London.

Although encouragement to use traffic-management techniques continued during the rest of the decade (in 1968, for example, such schemes were put on a comparable footing, for grant purposes, with structural improvements to primary highways), very severe criticism of the manner in which many schemes were implemented to the detriment of amenity reduced their attraction. By 1968, far from regarding traffic management as a means of trying to push more and more traffic through existing streets, the Ministry of Transport's advisory circular to local authorities on *Traffic and Transport Plans* referred instead to the need "to protect the environment by traffic management". Traffic management, rather than the total solution it had once been made to appear, became just one of a package of, largely complementary, remedies.

TRAFFIC RESTRAINT

If, as Plowden suggests, restriction of motorists in the 1950's and the concomitant need for discriminating were politically unacceptable, then circumstances must have brought about a change of attitude soon after. At the same time as the first experiments with comprehensive traffic management, tentative steps were being taken to restrict the use of cars in cities. It started with what has continued to remain the favoured method — parking controls; it started in London and in the following year, 1959, spread to the provinces with the implementation of the first provincial parking-meter scheme. This was only six years after a Ministry of Transport working party had concluded that the only answer (predictably in keeping with the "more of the same" philosophy) was more garages for off-street parking and under London's squares if need be, with the Ministry making good any deficits that "acceptable" charges to the motorist failed to cover.

By the time the idea that traffic was self-regulating had been discounted in the mid-1960's the traditional motor-car policy of rejecting restriction of use with its implied discrimination was in headlong retreat. In 1962 the Ministry had suggested ominously that alternatives might have to be considered to prevent private cars from unduly inflating peak-hour traffic jams, a view subsequently underlined by the Buchanan Report published in 1963. The Report acknowledged the possible need for restraint and suggested three ways of directly achieving this. These were: regulating road use by a system of permits, pricing directly the use of road space, and parking policy. Of these suggestions, the permit system was considered clumsy from an administrative viewpoint; the road-pricing solution was thought to be a long-term solution; the parking alternative was favoured as an immediately available measure. Meanwhile the alternatives were being subjected to more detailed examination by the panel on the economic and technical possibilities of road pricing, established under the chairmanship of Dr. Smeed in 1962. The report of this panel elucidated a number of ways of achieving restraint, based mainly on various uses of the pricing system, including differential fuel taxes, parking charges, differential licences of various types, and direct means of charging for the use of congested streets. The conclusions, published in 1964, were that parking taxes and a system of daily licences could bring significant benefits through restraint, but that a direct charging system was potentially the best solution. Following upon these conclusions, work began at the Road Research Laboratory in 1966 to study the feasibility of direct road-pricing systems and to develop the necessary equipment. To consider the operational opportunities for restraining traffic in the short term, the report of the Smeed panel was postscripted in the following year, 1965, by a Ministry of Transport Study Group. The deliberations of this group, published in 1967 under the title *Better Use of Town Roads*, reinforced the views of the Smeed panel. While direct road pricing seemed the most promising long-term approach to controlling the use of urban roads, parking restraint through parking controls was of the most value in the short term.

By the latter half of the 1960's the concept of deliberate restraint of city traffic had become established policy. The 1966 White Paper on *Transport Policy* made it clear that an effective traffic policy should also ensure that the volume of traffic entering congested areas is sensibly related to the capacity of the road system. It went on to draw the obvious conclusion that "this will require deliberate measures of traffic restraint". Eighteen months later, Roads Circular 1/68 called upon urban authorities to show in preparing their traffic and transport plans how they intended to relate their traffic and parking policies to the road capacities available — in other words, how they intended to restrain traffic.

The 1966 Government White Paper on *Transport Policy* concluded also that "at present, a thorough-going parking policy is the best method of restraint". Nevertheless, Mr. Marples had made the point in 1964 (a point which Mr. Peyton, Minister for Transport Industries, was to repeat seven years later) that it was up to the individual authorities to work out their own methods of controlling the car. In the event, although they, generally speaking, took action far more slowly and much less decisively than central government would have wished, local authorities appeared to have acted upon this advice of the 1966 White Paper. They looked to parking controls as the effective means of restraint.

PROMOTION OF PUBLIC TRANSPORT

Plowden (1971) has suggested restriction and restraint imply discrimination. Increasingly this has been practised in favour of public transport. At the opening of the 1960's, discussion of discrimination appeared to be centred upon the parking issue, with the resident and the short-term parker preferred to the longer-term commuter. This discussion later broadened and focused upon the point propagated with some feeling in the Buchanan Report that a distinction ought to be drawn between optional and essential traffic or, more loosely, between business and pleasure travel. The difficulty of giving substance to the terms optional and essential brought an end to serious discussion to these terms and attention turned around the middle of the decade to public transport and to the bus in particular. To some extent this was a consequence of the debate on the choice of methods of traffic restraint; politically, improved public transport was seen as the concomitant of general restriction on the use of other vehicles. The White Papers *Transport Policy* and *Public Transport and Traffic* illustrate the maturing of these views. Public transport now had a "key part to play in dealing with the urban transport problem" and in achieving "a better balance between the use of public transport and private cars" as a means of easing traffic congestion. "Transport plans must therefore be concerned with the interests of bus passengers *at least as much* as those who choose to use their own cars" (present writer's italics) and the duties of local authorities were to be redefined to include facilitating the passage of public service vehicles and securing the safety and convenience of persons using or desiring to use such vehicles.

To demonstrate how this could be achieved the Department of the Environment sponsored a number of technical trials and design studies of new systems of public transport. Notable amongst these were the special "partnership" studies first established with Leeds and later with Stevenage and the sponsoring of the Manchester Rapid Transit Study. This latter study was set up as a joint investigation with the Manchester Corporation in 1966 to examine various forms of rapid transit, including monorail, on a specified route between Ringway Airport, Wythenshawe, the City Centre, and Langley.

Towards the end of the decade discrimination in favour of public transport vehicles was no longer tacit. The Minister of Transport, Mr. Mulley, was by then overtly stating that "one solution . . . is to enable buses to defeat congestion by giving them special facilities and priorities over and above the normal run of traffic — special running lanes, priority at traffic lights, allowing them right-hand turns banned to other traffic and so on".

Changing attitudes were accompanied by changes in the financial and administrative constraints that in the evolving climate of opinion appeared to impose limitations or to reduce the incentive for local authorities to adopt new approaches to the urban-transport problem.

Prior to 1968 most of the Government's financial help towards local transport expenditure was concentrated on roads. Generally, it was administered in two ways. Either it was a specific grant — that is to say, it was paid for through a particular approved scheme of improvement (under the 1966 Local Government Act this was at the rate of 75% for principal roads) — or the contribution was through a non-specific Rate Support Grant, the amount of which was calculated for each local authority on the basis of a simple formula, taking into account (amongst other things) the mileage of road and the density of population. Improvements to non-principal roads and highway maintenance were supported in the latter way.

The bias towards private car transport inherent in the system ran counter to the policy, developing in the 1960's, of restraining the peak-hour use of the car in the larger urban areas and of promoting public transport. Consequently, the Government came to the conclusion that "investment in local public transport must be grant-aided by Central Government just as investment in the principal road network of our cities and towns receives capital grants of 75% from the Exchequer. Otherwise, the renewal and extension of public transport systems will be held up, while money available is concentrated on road schemes because they are grant-aided" (Ministry of Transport, 1967b).

In an attempt to effect this change of emphasis, the 1968 Transport Act introduced a number of new financial arrangements designed to help urban public transport. The chief ones were the infrastructure grants (under Section 56 of the Act) payable for approved expenditure on new fixed-track systems such as tube railways and busways (extended in 1971 to cover certain bus-priority schemes), on major improvements to existing rail systems, and on new or substantially improved interchange facilities (Table 3). There was also a specific grant for new buses (also increased in 1971) and for loss-making railway services in the major conurbations. But, in spite of this latter measure, the emphasis was very much upon capital spending on new public transport infrastructure, the basic intention being to balance the principal road grant by similar provision for public transport.

The administrative changes, intended to strike a new balance between public and private transport, centred first upon the setting up of the Passenger Transport Authorities in the major conurbations, under the 1968 Act, and upon the related transfer of London Transport to the GLC under the 1969 Transport (London) Act, a general move designed to institutionalise within local government structure a counterveiling force to the road planners. Hitherto, it was felt that the local authority had often had an interest in roads, and therefore the private motorist, but had had "little incentive to explore the development of rail and other rapid transit systems which might better serve local needs" (Ministry of Transport, 1966a, para. 58).

TABLE 3. Section 56 Transport Act 1968 and later amendments – Public Transport Infrastructure Grant Scheme

	Original scheme 8 August 1968		Extension to scheme 1 October 1971		Extension to scheme 22 November 1971		Extension to scheme 1 April 1972	
	Project	Grant rate (%)	Project	Grant rate (%)	Project	Grant rate (%)	Project	Grant rate (%)
Major Railway Projects e.g. New urban railway line or major improvement to an existing line. Grant may be paid in certain circumstances on rolling stock required for a new line or the electrification of an existing line		75	(a) Rolling stock: grants also towards cost of rehabilitating existing stock. (b) Signalling schemes included. (c) Improved systems of train control and automatic fare collection	75 75 75			In general, grants will no longer be paid on any railway project which costs less than £100,000 unless part of a group of projects costing over £100,000	
Railway Station Improvement Improvements at stations to improve their capacity or their convenience for passengers		50						
Area for Rail Projects Defined Basically GLC area and Passenger Transport areas							London area extended to coincide with BRB commuter network. PTE areas extended to 25 miles beyond boundaries	
Capital Improvement for Buses Special roads for buses and purpose-built bus lanes							From April 1971 50%. Now principal road schemes 75%. Non-principal road	

Bus Stations
Grants towards cost of bus station or improvement — 25

but applications should now state consideration given to pedestrian/vehicle safety within and on approach to station

Ferries
Provision or replacement of vessels. Improvement to ferry terminals — 50

New Forms of Transport
As for major railway projects

Bus Operation in Pedestrian Streets
Cost of highway improvements, e.g. traffic signs, signals, and road markings — 50

As with bus lanes, grants only payable if applicant authority spends £5000 or more on bus priority schemes

Bus Control Schemes
Grants payable to both bus control and mobile control equipment — 50

Note:

In addition to the grant scheme outlines above, a scheme which started 1 September 1968 made grants of 25% available for the purchase of new buses. The scheme was authorised for seven years under Section 32 of the Transport Act 1968. On 11 October 1971 the Minister for Transport Industries announced:

(a) The grants would be doubled to 50%.
(b) The scheme would be extended until 1980.

CHAPTER 4

Evaluation Policy

INTRODUCTION

The basic issue in modern transport planning is the need to choose carefully between alternative courses of action. It is a problem of choosing the "best", and the answer to the question of how we make better decisions has been that better choices will be made if comparison is carried out in a systematic manner.

Consistent choice between alternatives has generally been described as *maximisation subject to constraint*. When an individual chooses a car, for example, he may well attempt to maximise comfort or speed, or a combination of both of these, within the framework of constraints such as maximum price of £800, a certain degree of fuel economy, and so on. Approaching the subject in this way, it is necessary to decide what constraints are there, and above all what is it that has to be maximised, or, put another way, whose interest is the solution intended to serve? Clearly, these and related questions are essentially matters of public policy.

It is a hallmark of modern transport planning that both the constraints and the feature we maximise, which is usually termed the "objective function", are treated in the analysis explicitly and in a quantified form, which permits the development of criteria or tests of preferredness. The development of evaluation methods has certainly not excluded from a final consideration objectives which remain as yet unquantified. But these objectives are largely taken account of not as part of the systematic planning process, as here defined, but within the political process,[1] and as such act to modify the conclusions pointed to by systematic planning.

---

[1] This is taken to include the statutory planning inquiry procedure.

MAXIMISING THE OVERALL LEVEL OF SERVICE

The transport planner of the early sixties inherited from the highway planner a long tradition of narrowly defined but reasonably precise objective functions. In the context of the highway planner's general aim of improving the road system for the benefit of the traveller, vehicle speeds and road safety play important roles. "Journey speeds, running speeds, delays at intersections and accident information . . . give the measure of adequacy or otherwise of the roads concerned" was how one source of reference loosely put the point of view (Ministry of Transport, 1965).

The emphasis also was very much upon improving the situation at the time of most stress — the journey to work peak for the urban traveller, the August holiday month for the trunk-road user.[2]

Central to the theme was the idea of a road having a notional *capacity*. The consequence was that a level of vehicle flow on the highway *should* be catered for by a road network of suitable capacity if an acceptable speed was to be achieved. The road system should be continually improved to, and maintained at, that standard of efficiency. The crucial element in the approach became the normative judgement concerning the speed generally considered acceptable and some allowance was made for a variation in such expectations. One of the Ministry of Transport's manuals of guidance on these matters, *Roads in Urban Areas*, for example, made the point that "the speed of traffic in towns will be lower than that on rural roads and there will be less overtaking; *drivers are prepared for these conditions* and higher traffic densities can therefore be allowed" (present writer's italics).

This approach was originally intended for assisting with the design of roads, either new roads or improvements to existing ones, and only comparatively recently was it adapted for choosing between alternative proposals. One outcome was the engineers' overload criterion which expressed the realised or expected flow of traffic as a ratio of the road capacity (Ministry of Transport, 1966b, para. 4.3). In these circumstances the choice of the best plan became a matter of choosing that which minimised

---

[2] The tradition is strong in the USA where the 1950 *Highway Capacity Manual* states that with certain caveats "the thirtieth highest hourly volume for the year is generally a reliable criterion of the needed capacity . . .". A similar view that "The design of main traffic routes in built-up areas should be based on peak-hour demands and not, as in rural areas, on average daily flow during August" is expressed in Ministry of Transport (1966b).

the degree of overload on the transport network within the limits of the transport budget.

In spite of the successful adaptation of the original design criteria to this new task, at the time that the systems approach to transport planning was evolving in Britain a concurrent and profound change in policy was taking place with respect to the type of objective function the planner was required to maximise. At first the change was not so much in terms of whose interest was being maximised — essentially the same general interests were being secured (the perception of the transport problem was not markedly different). But the difference was in terms of the way in which the objective function was expressed and calculated. Influenced by the adoption for planning purposes of a fixed or restricted transport resource budget (see page 17), this policy has been the general adoption of economic criteria with the constraints in the form of costs and the surplus of advantage maximised in the form of an economic rent.[3]

MAXIMISING PROFITS

The expression of policy objectives in planning matters in more precise economic terms is generally regarded as being synonymous with the application of social cost—benefit analysis, but a social maximand is not a necessary condition of pursuing an economic objective. A policy of maximising profits, in more popular terms commercialism, fulfils the required conditions and is used as a basis for choosing between alternative courses of action in transport, e.g. by the nationalised transport industries. But there are difficulties of applying it as the basis of an overall planning criterion.

Maximising profits (producers' surplus, to use the economic jargon) requires an effective pricing policy producing a flow of cash from any new facility, or from any change made to the transport system. There are problems involved here where a combination of practical issues, custom, and political viewpoint resulted in certain sections of transport not being subject to the necessary rigours of an effective pricing system — the villain of the piece being the highway user.

---

[3] See in particular Foster (1963) for an elaboration of this argument. The general theme of economic evaluation is comprehensively covered in Harrison (1974).

The difficulty of and objections to running the highway system in this way has not, none the less, prevented some in recent times from taking an essentially commercial view of highway improvements. Evidence put before the 1905 Royal Commission on London's Traffic argued that "about three times the area of land actually required for road construction should be taken, and the surplus resold at its improved value to recoup the major part, if not all, of the initial outlay". A number of local authority planning documents in the pre-war and early post-war years reveal a similar commercial acumen, setting out their case as a financial profit and loss account from the viewpoint of the local authority. *The Preliminary Draft Proposals for Post-war Reconstructions in the City of London* (1944) are a case in point, where reference is made to the benefits accruing from enhanced property values. More specifically and much more recently, the Chairman of the Birmingham Public Works Committee made the same point in reference to Birmingham's Inner Ring Road. He put it thus: "There is also the more tangible benefit received from leasing the surplus frontage land, and the increased rateable value of the new properties compared with the old properties. . . ." (Fig. 4.)

Clearly, therefore, to determine what is appropriate the planning process starts with a value judgement — *whose interest is to be served?* If it is to be the interests of those who provide the transport facility, the Corporation of Birmingham as in the example given above, then the approach will be a "commercial" one of profit maximisation or some derivative thereof. But any investment, or any change in the practices of operating the transport system, can be viewed as serving the interests of other (specified) sections of the community; in this case the basis of the appropriate criterion will be to maximise their particular economic rent or surplus of their benefit over their costs.

MAXIMISING USER SURPLUSES

The viewpoint, that changes to the transport system ought to be evaluated in terms which specify the effect on economic rents other than producers' rents, has a long history. The arguments are generally recognised as stemming from Dupuit's writings in the middle of the last century. In his work published in 1844 Dupuit argued that the total satisfaction resulting from the construction of something like a bridge or canal was greater than

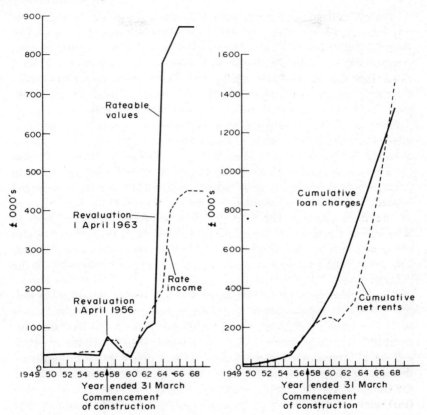

FIG. 4. Cash flow (loan charges and rents from adjacent property) of Birmingham's inner ring road (Smallbrook Ringway Section) (Thomas, 1963).

the direct revenues which would be obtained because many of the customers would have been willing to pay more rather than go without the service. He considered that this surplus of satisfaction (or net benefit) should be taken into account. Dupuit was mainly concerned with the implications of this consumers' surplus for the levying of tolls, but his case also has an obvious bearing on an appropriate policy for investment. Indeed, it is not generally appreciated that such ideas were put into practice before the publication of Dupuit's treatise.

In the United Kingdom after 1820 the calculation of the change in the consumers' surplus enjoyed by travellers, expressed in terms of the reduction in effort required to pull vehicles consequent upon decreasing gradients, became a principal design consideration for engineers (Paxton, 1969). Such a procedure was used about 1830 by Macneill, one of Telford's engineers working on the Holyhead road. The results of his Stowe Hill Valley assessment were based upon the expense of drawing one ton by stagecoach over four miles (weighted for the daily traffic tonnage) for five competing (or mutually exclusive) proposals.

This century the stimulus came from the United States where, with the New Deal, the idea developed of broader social justification for projects. Such ideas soon spread to the transport planning field and the State of Oregon conducted much experimental work at the end of the 1930's.

In Great Britain such ideas of calculating the net user benefits of transport projects do not appear to have been taken up again until the latter half of the 1950's. A method for the economic assessment of road improvement schemes was first put forward by the Government Road Research Laboratory in draft form in 1956. The Road Research Board then set up a special panel of engineers serving with local authorities to try out the draft method on specific schemes.

An interim statement of these ideas appeared in a paper presented to the Institute of Civil Engineers Conference on the Highway Needs of Great Britain in 1957 by Glanville, then Head of the Road Research Laboratory, and his colleague Smeed. This was followed in 1960 by a Road Research Laboratory Technical Paper on the *Assessment of Priority for Road Improvements*. At the same time, what is now regarded as the seminal work on British transport cost—benefit analysis, the London—Birmingham Motorway (M1) study, was being conducted for the Laboratory. This was an analysis concurrent with the building of the motorway, but it did prove a most useful exercise in adapting to British conditions and circumstances the earlier American analyses.

The items of cost and benefit, which formed the core of the calculations of the net annual savings the project would bring are illustrated in Table 4.

Although the M1 study may appear to give the same order of importance to road-users as do the earlier technical appraisals, there were differences. Firstly, there is less emphasis upon those using the transport

TABLE 4. The incidence of estimated savings (−) and increases (+) in
annual costs resulting from construction of the London−Birmingham
Motorway

	Changes in £000's per annum		
	First assignment	Second assignment	Third assignment
Savings in working time by traffic transferring to motorway	−453	−624	−766
Reduction in vehicle fleets	− 80	−161	−227
Change in fuel consumption for vehicle-mileage transferred to motorway	−117	− 84	− 18
Change in other operating costs for vehicle-mileage transferred	−200	−200	−200
Costs of additional vehicle-mileage incurred in transferring to motorway	+229	+307	+375
Reductions in cost to vehicles remaining on old roads	−128	−128	−128
Total vehicle costs	−749	−890	−964
Reduction in accidents	−215	−215	−215
Maintenance costs of motorway	+200	+200	+200
Net annual measured savings	−764	−905	−979

Notes: (1) The three assignments represent different assumptions regarding motorway driving speeds.
          (2) Where appropriate, the items are net of tax.

system at peak times and secondly, the various components of traffic are
weighted differently.

From such bases the Ministry began to develop procedures for general
application, particularly to road schemes. The first development along
such lines was a hybrid of economic and technical approaches, known as
TAL (Travel and Accident Loss) used for trunk-road planning in the mid-
1960's. TAL was the difference between operating costs and accident costs
as they actually were on existing roads and what those costs would be if
the road was built to the Ministry's modern standards of design for new

roads. The method was based on the supposition that the design standard was optimum and in this context TAL per vehicle was regarded as providing "an indication of the quality of a road in terms of its liability to give rise to congestion" (Ministry of Transport, 1966c, para. 4.5).

Concurrently, the Ministry was progressively developing procedures to enable it to identify the location, type, and timing of schemes which offered the highest returns — "and thus the highest economic benefits to the community" (Ministry of Transport, 1966c, para. 4.6). The outcome was Technical Memorandum 5 issued in 1967. T5/67, as it was known, required the calculation, using standard unit values, of savings in travel time, in operating costs, in accident costs, and the presentation of the results as a one-year rate of return on capital costs. The proforma issued was recommended for use in the assessment of rural road schemes. Although some of the techniques were rather elementary and crude and suffered from inevitable standardisation associated with any proforma, nevertheless T5/67 established the use of a user surplus objective function in transport planning.

MAXIMISING THE COMBINED SURPLUS OF USERS AND OPERATORS

In the case of highways tradition or other reasons had meant that, for the most part, such facilities were provided freely. Therefore, in the analysis of new highway investments the interests of the user had been the principal if not the sole concern. With other types of facilities, tradition, however, did not necessarily favour the user to the same extent. In these other instances there were the interests of the producer or operator to be taken into account and consequently the procedure was not simply one of maximising the surpluses of consumers.

This difference of approach, when revenues were extracted from users, was illustrated by the Ministry of Transport's study of *Proposals for a Fixed Channel Link* (Ministry of Transport, 1963b). In this particular case three mutually exclusive systems of crossing the English Channel — a bridge, a tunnel, and an improvement, albeit limited, of then-existing cross-Channel services — were compared. Because of the commercial aspects of the proposals, in certain respects the analysis differed from the London—Birmingham Motorway analysis. For example, traffic diverted from established means was presumed to benefit solely from the reduction in total transport costs reflected in lower crossing tolls. (Unlike the London—Birmingham Motorway study, no allowance was made for the value of possible savings in travel time.)

> For traffic generated by the fixed link [the study] examined the position from the point of view of the operator and of the users in turn, in order to assess the corresponding benefits. For the users, on average this benefit, which may be described as the "users' surplus", is approximately equal to half the difference between the charge for the established means of transport and the charge that would be carried on the fixed crossing. For the operator, the generated traffic yields benefits equal to his additional receipts after deduction of his additional costs.

These latter benefits were, of course, additional profits to the operator or producer of the fixed Channel link (Table 5).

Towards the end of the 1960's, with increased emphasis being placed upon promoting public transport, the commercial viability of which had always been of importance, this aspect of an operator's surplus took on added significance. Section 56 of the Transport Act of 1968, for example, provided for the Minister of Transport to make grants towards capital expenditure on public transport facilities and this encouraged the Ministry to develop procedures for evaluating revenue-earning investments.

Moreover, another significant section in the 1968 Act resulted in revision of the financial constraints on railway operations and reduced the need for proposals to be self-liquidating. Section 39 of the Act provided for the Minister of Transport to undertake to pay a grant towards loss-making railway services where this was deemed desirable for economic and social reasons.

As a consequence, there was less emphasis upon evaluation procedures aiming to maximise user surplus, subject to some minimum financial return, and more emphasis upon maximising the combined surpluses of user and operator. This change is apparent if one compares the 1963 Channel Crossing analysis with, for example, the Government's analysis of British Railways' proposal at the end of the decade to upgrade, with the aid of a Section 56 grant, the lines from King's Cross to Hertford and Royston (Table 6).

In this latter case two rail alternatives, electrification and "super-diesel", were compared with a base situation where the then-existing service was maintained by replacing like-for-like. The comparison was in

TABLE 5. Evaluation of a fixed Channel link. "Upper" and "lower" traffic estimates, all figures adjusted to 1969 values and represent differences from a base case of established means. (Adapted from Ministry of Transport, 1963b)

	Upper		Lower	
	Tunnel	Bridge	Tunnel	Bridge
	£ millions (rounded figures)			
1. Producer's costs and benefits (a) Reduced capital and operating expenses	+240	+235	+289	+182
(b) Additional revenue from generated traffic	+ 47	+ 61	+ 23	+ 31
Total	+287	+296	+312	+213
2. User benefits (a) Benefits to new users attracted by the improvement	+ 7	+ 9	+ 3	+ 5
Total	+ 7	+ 9	+ 3	+ 5
3. Initial capital cost	−141	−351	−141	−352
Overall net benefit	+153	− 46	+174	−134

TABLE 6. Evaluation of Great Northern suburban rail services [all figures are
differences from "base" (like-for-like replacement).
Expenditure Committee (1972), Appendix 3]

		Electrification		"Super-diesel"	
		£ millions			
1. Rail-user (direct benefits)	(a) Time savings to existing users	+3.6		+2.5	
	(b) Time savings to additional users expected whether service improved or not	+0.3		+0.2	
	(c) Benefits to new users attracted by improvement	+0.7		+0.3	
	Total		+4.6		+3.0
2. Road-user (indirect benefits)	(a) Reduction in costs to remaining road-users, with allowance for benefit to new users attracted by congestion relief		+8.8		+6.7
3. Producer's costs and benefits (LT and BR)	(a) Additional revenue to BR	+3.3		+1.8	
	(b) Increase in working expenses to BR	−0.8		−4.1	
	(c) Net savings to LT from transfer of Northern City line	+2.7		Nil	
	Total		+5.2		−2.3
4. Capital costs (incremental)			−8.2		−3.3
Net benefit			+10.4		+4.1

terms of the effects on the users of both rail and competing road facilities
and upon the cash-flow margins of British Railways and London Transport. The analysis showed that one particular option, super-diesels, would
result in a deteriorating financial situation for British Railways in spite of
an overall surplus. Electrification, however, produced a larger surplus and
some measure of net benefits for all interests considered.

SURPLUS CHANGES TO NON-USERS

It is generally recognised that there may be changes of surplus either in the form of profits or of satisfactions to persons or institutions not using the transport system in a direct manner. This is not to argue that these particular sections of the community will never, for example, use the transport system and thus never enjoy or suffer changes in user surplus, but merely to point out that an alteration in the system may impose changes on certain persons even while they are not actually in the process of moving from place to place.

Until recently, the non-users' surplus elements generally have been ignored in the "official" appraisal of planned changes to the transport system. This happened for two main reasons. Firstly, there was considerable doubt that there existed any non-user costs and benefits not already taken account of in the calculation of net benefits to users and operators of the transport system. The comparatively greater increase in the price of housing in the vicinity of a newly opened motorway, for example, is said to merely reflect the savings of time and wear and tear to motorists. To include both the increase in property values and the changed costs of travel to road-users would be, in these circumstances, to count the same thing twice. The generally recognised exception to this rule has been the amenity implications of transport developments — noise, fumes, and visual intrusion.

The second reason hinges upon McKean's (1958) point that many shadow prices are not (politically) worth estimating, a view echoing Foster's (1963) comment that "we may not wish to put some social benefit or cost in, quite simply because we do not wish to consider it. . . . To generalise, the effects of any choice can be divided into three groups, (i) the good . . . , (ii) the bad, (iii) the indifferent. Whoever is responsible for making the decision is responsible for defining 'good', 'bad' and 'indifferent'." In the process of focusing upon the gain to the transport-user the decision-makers have chosen, it would appear, to treat many side-effects in an indifferent manner.

One could detect a definite shift of opinion late in the 1960's, however, and the independent Third London Airport Commission interpreted the reference to cost–benefit analysis in its brief in a broader sense. The Commission said, for example, that "one of the advantages of the cost benefit approach to site assessment is that *all* the important factors are thoroughly considered ..." (present writer's italics) and the study made a thorough analysis of many non-user elements, particularly in the field of amenity where the disturbance to residents, schools, hospitals, commerce, and persons recreating were all taken into account in monetary terms.

THE TREATMENT OF INTANGIBLES

A further change of attitude in the later sixties was also to be seen in the explicit consideration of certain items of costs and benefit which defied expression in money terms. In spite of the Third London Airport Commission's notable attempts to extend cost—benefit analysis in this direction, it remains true that many items are not susceptible to such rigorous treatment. Indeed, the Commission themselves did not explicitly value in money terms the loss of wild life and churches, the regional planning factors, or the value of preserving the countryside, all of which had some bearing on the final decision (1971, para. 12.7).

But an apparent change of opinion is registered by a greater willingness at least to list such factors thought to be relevant to the decision. This is well illustrated in the Cambrian Coast Line Report (Ministry of Transport, 1969b), where the items shown in Table 7 were listed for consideration.

The nature of this approach was extended still further in the *Report of a Study of Rail Links with Heathrow Airport* (Ministry of Transport, 1970a) by the treatment given to the non-pecuniary features of the alternatives, in this case a British Railways link with variations in check-in facilities, supplementary coach services, and an extension to the London Transport Executives' Piccadilly Line (Table 8).

The point of view that emerged was that "while cost—benefit calculations are necessary, they are not sufficient and need to be accompanied by a description of other factors" (National Board for Prices and Incomes, 1970).

Nevertheless, unless these other factors are capable of clear definition and are positively identifiable in an objective function, they do not justify *thorough* treatment within the systematic planning process. Such a definition depends upon the political process treating them with a degree of importance that makes, to repeat McKean's point, the shadow prices worth estimating. Although there were signs of a change at the end

TABLE 7. Intangible benefits and costs of retaining the rail service along the Cambrian coast

Benefits	Costs
1. Higher standard of comfort which would be lost if passengers transferred to buses.	1. Less attractive bus service due to present low traffic.
2. Avoidance of job-changing and associated disruption for those using line for journeys to work.	2. Disruption of local road movement across the railway at level crossings.
3. Higher output of tourist industry (assuming some present rail travellers would not be replaced by those travelling by bus or car).	
4. Emergency access across estuaries (if railway bridges were dismantled and replaced).	
5. Explosives traffic kept off roads.	
6. Possible advantage in industrial development prospects.	

TABLE 8. Rail links with Heathrow Airport. Factors affecting choice of link which were not included in the cost—benefit calculations

Factor	BR1	BR2	BR3	LT
Choice of two public modes	No	Yes	Yes	Yes
Option of check-in in Central London for rail-link passengers	Yes	Yes	No	No
Comfort	Good	Good	Good	Fair/Good
Baggage handling	Very good*	Very good*	Fair/Good	Fair
Reliability	Good	Good	Good	Very good
Town planning	Acceptable	Acceptable	Acceptable	Acceptable

*Assuming a reliable system can be developed.

of the 1960's until this time (with the exception of the Third London Airport Study) the political process did not appear to endow the secondary costs and benefits with this necessary significance.

THE DISTRIBUTION OF SURPLUSES BETWEEN CONTEMPORARIES

So far we have seen how evaluation policy has been formulated in terms of maximising some surplus of value and how this surplus has been defined differently in various studies with regard to whose surplus has been given priority. Society, operating through the political process, has decided that some surpluses are worth maximising and others are not, and so far the focus of attention has been the motorist, or the operator of rail services, and so on. But there is a further way in which value judgements concerning surpluses might have been made, and this is by valuing pounds differently depending upon who is the recipient. In other words, policy might operate not just by saying that some surpluses are important and therefore shall be counted, but by suggesting that of those which do count, some count more than others.

Discussion of this issue draws a distinction between recipients not only in terms of their activities, which has tended to be the focus up to now, but in terms of the income or wealth of the persons concerned. Thus a distinction might be made between the poor car-driver and the rich car-driver, between the wealthy person injured in an accident and the less wealthy. In practice, policy has not operated in such an overt manner and any distinction measured in terms of income or wealth has been implied, largely in terms of the valuation of various items of cost and benefit involved in the estimation of the surplus of value, and through the valuation of travel time in particular.

The basis of most time valuation is empirical — that is to say, it is based upon an actual market in the case of working time and an inferred market situation in the case of non-working time, these being derived from situations where people make choices which imply values for time. In the field of transport the use of a tolled estuary crossing where its use involves a higher expenditure in return for a quicker journey provides evidence that people value time. Similarly, in many large cities choices exist between various modes of transport which have different speed and cost (or fare) characteristics and which, therefore, allow the expression of a preference for the more expensive but quicker mode.

Nevertheless, there remain certain areas of time-saving which cannot be valued in this way, and it fell to those making decisions on these matters to decide whether to ignore such aspects completely or to ascribe an arbitrary value. In some cases arbitrary values of time are applied to travel activity — e.g. leisure journeys as opposed to journeys to and from the place of work. In other instances these policy values can be interpreted as having an equity implication where the pounds of some social groups are weighed differently from those of others. The decision to value children's time at one-third of the rate for adults and the decision to value house-wives' time at the same rate as that of earning adults, on the basis that "in the modern family it seems reasonable to assume that the husband would be prepared to see his wife pay as much as he to save time" (Ministry of Transport, 1969c) could be interpreted in the equity context.

But whatever the opinion on these points, the question of equity does affect unequivocally the valuation of time in another way. Although there is evidence that the value placed upon time savings varies with the income of the persons concerned and that different groups of travellers have different incomes, it is currently official policy to use only one value for leisure time saved, regardless of the circumstances.

> *The main reason for this is a simple equity consideration.* Road use is not paid for directly by road users in the sense that if a new road is provided, no extra charge is normally levied for it. To employ a higher value of time for higher income groups results in a diversion of expenditure towards schemes used by such groups, but no corresponding payment by them. (Ministry of Transport, 1969c. Present writer's italics.)

This particular embodiment of equity became known as the social value of time.

This issue of the proper distribution of a surplus amongst contemporaries is to be seen in an increasing tendency to present the surplus, the net benefit of the various alternatives considered, in a disaggregated manner which allows those making the final decision to apply their own particular weightings to the pounds received by different groups of persons. A breakdown in terms of journey, activity, or nature of the benefit, disbenefit, or cost is, of course, fairly traditional and is seen in the tables presenting the nature of the earlier economic appraisals already shown in this chapter.

Less traditional is a breakdown of the surplus according to geographical areas as introduced in the London Transportation Study and repeated in the more recent South-east Study.

DISTRIBUTION OVER TIME

Besides considering which surpluses (and therefore which benefits and costs, advantages and disadvantages) to take into account, and how the emphasis given to each surplus might differ according to whose surplus it is, there is a further aspect to consider. The advantages and disadvantages of carrying out any proposal are felt not at a single point in time but over a period of time, which in many cases can be a very long period running over a number of decades. Indeed, at the time decisions are made, those most seriously affected may not even have been born. How then are we to treat the surpluses of future time periods in comparison with those arising in a more immediate context?

The starting-point is usually taken to be the measure of the community's view of the value of extra consumption (in the sense of an increment to the *general* living standard) in the future as compared with the present. The measure of this value is defined as a rate of discount r which makes the persons involved equally satisfied with $£(1 + r)^n$ worth of extra consumption in any future year n as with £1 worth in the present. It can be argued, of course, that in the context of choosing between well-defined and not too dissimilar alternative courses of action, with similar timings of advantage and disadvantage (the Third London Airport choice being a case in point), the problem of choosing an appropriate value for the rate of discount does not really matter. And it is generally true that in transport, unlike the electricity supply industry, for example, the phasing of the alternative projects and their associated advantages and disadvantages is very similar.

This seems a perfectly reasonable argument provided we take a rather blinkered view of the situation and are concerned only with choosing the "best" from a number of alternatives examined at a particular time in a particular study. But, if we pose a different question, "Is the 'best' good enough?", or to put it another way, "Should we go ahead with the selected alternatives?", then the rate of discount amongst other factors does begin to matter. In these circumstances we are implying a comparison not only with other transport plans but with the possible uses of resources in other sectors of the economy, and in this context the appropriate rate of discount becomes a measure of these other "opportunities".

In practice, "sub-optimisation" has been the rule. The budget that transport-planners have faced as a constraint has been fixed by the political process. Nor was there any guidance on such matters as the appropriate rates of discount to be used. In these circumstances it is perhaps understandable that in the past the transport-planning process, faced with the issue of choosing between alternatives with very similar timings, chose to disregard one of two dimensions that any commitment of resources may possess — namely, its timing.

Nearly all of the early economic appraisals of road schemes calculated the net benefits for one year, which in some cases was the first year the road was expected to be open, and in other cases some fixed period after the opening of the road, or as with the case of the Ministry of Transport's Memorandum to local authorities (Technical Memorandum T5/67) for a specific year (1974). In each case, one pound's worth of surplus was regarded as having the same value regardless of when it accrued.

In the late 1960's, however, and with more positive guidance from the central planning authorities, a change of emphasis began to occur. With the publication in 1967 of the White Paper *Nationalised Industries: a review of economic and financial objectives* the nationalised industries were given definite encouragement to carry out what is termed a discounted cash-flow appraisal of their proposed capital investment programmes. Within this context, the Treasury recommended a test rate of discount of 8%, a rate which at the time represented "the minimum rate of return to be expected on a marginal low-risk project undertaken for commercial reasons".

The 1967 White Paper provided the incentive for the Ministry of Transport to encourage a similar approach in the field of transport planning and to adopt the Treasury's rate of discount. This encouragement came in 1968 when the MoT expressed the view:

Although in some cases a first year rate of return gives an adequate guide, it is more often the case that benefits and costs over the life of the scheme must be considered, using discounting techniques to relate sums in the various years. (Ministry of Transport, 1968b.)

The following year in evidence to the inquiry into Motorways and

Trunk Roads by the House of Commons Estimates Committee, the Ministry clarified its attitude:

> Since the benefits derived will vary substantially over the life of a scheme (and in different ways for different schemes) it is an improvement in the technique to calculate the rate of return by establishing costs and benefits over a period (30 years) and discounting them to a base year. . . . The Department has developed and used on a limited scale a computer program for this and is engaged in developing the general procedures to make it the normal method of calculating the cost/benefit of road schemes. (Estimates Committee, 1969.)

Thus, by the end of the decade the focus of attention had changed from one year's surplus of benefit to the surpluses accruing over a substantial period of time.

CONCLUSIONS

In this chapter we have been considering what may loosely be called the evaluation procedures in transport planning. In so doing, we have considered at length what constitutes to a very large degree the content of a phase which is close to terminating the typical planning study, and as such, it could be said that we have digressed into the realm of cost—benefit analysis and other aspects of evaluation.

But this is a very necessary digression. The point is a simple one. If, when it is applied, the planning process is to be internally consistent in all its facets, it must start by considering the context of the study: to do this it must refer to a framework provided by current policy, and policy impinges most directly upon evaluation by determining *what* shall count and *how* it shall be counted. This has been the purpose of this synoptic review of both policy statements on matters of evaluation and the evaluation within past transport planning studies as they were practised.

The review shows that policy on these matters did change in the 1960's and it was incumbent upon the transport-planner to take account of these changes in his analysis and indeed to make sure that the manner of his evaluation and methods of his analysis were consistent. Whether he did so is the subject of the next chapter.

CHAPTER 5

Transportation Planning Models

MATHEMATICAL SIMULATION: THE TRAVEL MODEL

Modern transport planning grew from a realisation in America during the early 1950's that traffic was a function of land use (and, though this was less appreciated, that land use in turn was a function of traffic). There was a growing appreciation too that a facile expansion of the existing travel pattern, based upon the anticipated growth in the national economy or in the number of cars owned, was a most inadequate approach to the planning of new transport facilities. Instead, a method was required for predicting the consequences to travel patterns of changing patterns of development in cities. At first in Detroit and Chicago, and later in other metropolitan areas, a number of theories collectively termed the travel model were evolved.

These made it possible to predict the changes that would result from new road networks and new systems of organisation such as traffic management so that a strategy for choosing between alternative solutions to problems such as traffic congestion slowly emerged with the travel model forming a crucial phase in the evolution of this planning process. This standard process became known as the transportation study.

Traditionally, the travel model is made up of four component parts or sub-models, the output of one forming the input of the next in the sequence. Information about transport networks, about the location of activities, and about characteristics of households such as income or number of cars owned is introduced into the model sequence,[1] while the output

---

[1] This information itself is in part the outcome of developing models; of these, only models of car-ownership have been traditionally the responsibility of transport-planners. For a comprehensive account of the mathematical structure of transport models see Lane *et al.* (1971) and Hutchinson (1974).

which effectively represents the simulated workings of the transport system is used as a basis for a subsequent evaluation phase. The *implicit* conceptional foundations of the traditional travel model are that the decisions made by the traveller follow a simple sequence; having decided to undertake a journey, he then proceeds to choose his mode of transport, his journey destination, and finally his precise route. This sequence is reflected in the classical structure of the model with its travel-generation, modal-split, trip-distribution, and route-assignment stages.

This basic travel model which evolved in the 1950's at the scale of the North American metropolis formed the basis of nearly all subsequent transport planning studies. In this country the model-building aspects of the Third London Airport inquiry, the report of the Portbury Dock Study and the national highway network model, referred to in the 1969 Green Paper on inter-urban roads, all, in spite of their ex-urban context and emphasis, lean heavily upon this generic base.

Estimating the Number of Journeys Made

The fundamental assumption of the theories and processes evolved in Chicago and Detroit is that there exists a reasonably stable relationship between the uses of land — industrial, commercial, public open space, and residential — and the demands for transport services. Over the years this focus upon land use as the basis of trip-making has been modified by the greater emphasis upon the notion of urban activities and their traffic and transport implications. Nevertheless, the rudiments of the method remain essentially the same.

At the core of the analysis lies the household. The objective of the early American and British studies was to improve the technical efficiency and reliability of the transport system from the point of view of the users. With this aim in view the criteria of those studies were essentially of a technical nature (although the Chicago study in the later 1950's experimented with the use of simple economic measures of efficiency). They placed stress on the performance of the system at times of maximum usage, namely during the journey-to-work peak and its late afternoon reciprocal. This in turn led to emphasis on residential land use as the basis of urban trip-making and consequently most of the model-building took place in this context. In spite of the changing nature of the objective function this remained the position throughout the 1960's.

The early models were based upon two aspects: on the one hand a fairly simple classification of trips from residential areas according to their purpose, the most important category of which was the work journey, and on the other hand an explanation of the frequency of these journeys in terms of the areas' residential characteristics. Studies indicated that of many factors, family size, car-ownership, income, and occupational status appeared to be most closely related to the frequency of trips made. Other variables shown in the earlier studies to have an influence on trip frequency summarised the locational characteristics of the areas in such terms as distance from the centre of the city.[2]

There were dangers in this method, however, due largely to the emphasis which was being placed on identifying a statistical measure of association between trip-making and residential characteristics. In many cases the factors in the study were indicators of the same or related things, e.g. car-ownership, occupation, and income, and simply to demonstrate correlations, as many studies did, told us little about the true factors which influence people's behaviour.[3]

A second criticism was levelled at the use of area-based statistics (usually aggregated to the scale of the traffic zone), which meant that the models explained the variations in trip-making between respective *areas* but not between *households* which they often purported to do. As explanations of future trip-making behaviour they depended upon the fragile assumption that the amount of variation in trip behaviour within the area would remain in constant ratio to the variation between different areas.[4]

Developments in some of the later transport-planning studies[5] attempted to overcome these drawbacks. New lines of approach investigated included studies to determine the factors which condition trip-making deci-

[2] As in the *Leicester Traffic Plan* (1963–4) and the *Belfast Transportation Plan* (1965–9).

[3] These technical criticisms of trip-generation models are expounded in relation to American studies by W. Oi and P. Shuldiner (1962), and more recently in this country by A. Douglas and R. Lewis (1971). The interested reader is referred to these sources.

[4] A good example of model-building subject to serious criticism on both these grounds is the *Cardiff Development and Transportation Study* (1966–8), which incorporated into an area analysis of residential trip-generation, population, number of households, number of employed residents, numbers of cars owned, and the area of residential land.

[5] Belfast, West Midlands, SELNEC.

sions among household members without reference to their area of residence (Fig. 5). As a consequence the locational characteristics, introduced into the earlier explanation of trip-making, disappeared from the more recent studies.

This consequence was not without significance, however, in view of the increasing emphasis placed by policy towards the end of the 1960's decade upon traffic restraint. One would expect the movements of people to be affected by the ease with which they could move around. For example, the building of a motorway or the restriction of traffic in city centres could be expected to have a number of different but related repercussions on travel behaviour. Persons might change their mode of travel, they might

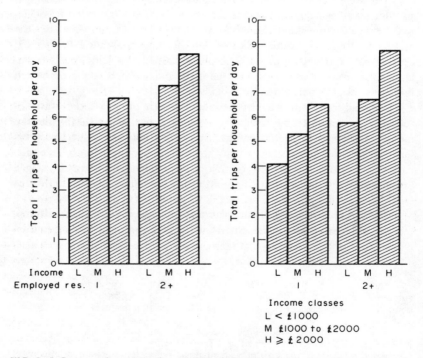

FIG. 5. Influence of number of employed residents and income on trip generation in the West Midlands Transportation Study (left) and the London Traffic Survey.

change their journey's destination, and last, but not least, we could expect them to alter the frequency with which they undertook journeys. It is this last aspect which is pertinent here.

To an extent the earlier model-building had taken account of this problem through the incorporation of location as a factor determining the number of journeys undertaken by a household. A measure such as distance from the city centre, for example, would reflect congestion and therefore accessibility in so far as these effects could be argued to vary systematically by area. None of the later urban studies, however, compensated for the absence of such factors by incorporating any direct measure of accessibility.[6]

The significance of this is profound, illustrating as it does the failure of the model-building to keep pace with evolving policy. With the early emphasis on technical criteria and simple measures of the level of service provided by the transport networks, the problem did not really arise. The nature of the methods used was such that the proposals were expected to answer the travel demands that would arise at some future date provided absolute accessibility remained similar to that prevailing at the time of the planning study. The fact that this approach depended on a curious logic, that the existence of the planned roads was a pre-supposition of the flows they were intended to facilitate, at least avoided the accessibility problem in model-building.

But policy evolved in two ways, both of which highlight this particular weakness in transport-modelling. First, as we noted in Chapter 1, there was the general acceptance of the systematic comparison of alternatives as the fulcrum of the "new" transport-planning. Increasingly this comparison was made in terms of economic criteria with the concept of "doing nothing" providing a bench-mark. In other words, it had become necessary to know how much travel would take place in future years if the present network remained fundamentally in its present state. With the expansion of travel, this implies a more congested network and therefore *decreasing* accessibility.

Secondly, policy has called forth the examination and consideration of options incorporating the use of the present system in a more "efficient" manner, implying in most cases the need to examine and test the effects

---

[6] Outside the urban context the sole exception was the surface-access model used by the research team in the Third London Airport Study.

on travel behaviour of positive measures of restraint either in the form of parking controls or, increasingly, in terms of road-congestion pricing. As one government report puts it, "the key point about parking is that its presence or absence at the terminal point of urban journeys influences the way in which people travel".

Both of these changes made necessary some method of showing the relationship between trip-making and accessibility. In this respect in the 1960's trip-generation models, if they changed at all, regressed rather than progressed.

There was a further weakness of trip-generation methods highlighted by policy developments in the 1960's. It was reasoned earlier in this chapter that the emphasis upon technical criteria such as the degree of "overload" at times of peak usage led to a concentration of early model development upon household travel. The partial neglect of other components of urban travel such as business journeys and movements by goods vehicles, and even weekend household travel, gathered significance with the growing importance of economic criteria during the 1960's. It was pointed out in Chapter 4 that the economic criteria were in a sense selective in so far as they sought to measure the surpluses and benefits to certain sections of the community. This selectivity, nevertheless, did not extend, as the technical criteria had done more fundamentally, to discriminate between persons and institutions making use of the roads at certain time periods and therefore to discriminate tacitly between the purposes for which journeys were made. In other words, the benefits received by business travellers and goods-vehicle operators were now to count equally in importance with those benefits enjoyed by the daily commuter. Model-building during the decade failed to reflect this trend in policy. Whereas the theories of household travel were increasingly refined, similar refinement with respect to other types of travel was singularly absent.[7]

The point is straightforward. The technical criticism of trip-generation models made by Shuldiner, Douglas and others apply equally to journeys dissociated from residential activities. In spite of this and in spite of the

---

[7] In *Traffic in the Conurbations* (Alan M. Voorhees *et al.*, 1971) it is argued that this state of affairs was principally the result of limited money available for survey work so that studies were forced to minimise the efforts on goods-traffic analysis. But there is little evidence that transport-planners stressed the importance of a successful goods model to the commissioning bodies.

development of household trip models to meet many of their critics' points, all business travel and all movement of goods were explained without exception in the 1960's by the use of area statistics. Journeys made were related in most cases simply to total employment.

The Use and Choice of Mode

With the anticipated levels of car-ownership, it was assumed in the North American planning studies of the 1950's that public-transport use would become an incidental feature of city life. By concentrating exclusively upon options and alternatives that represented variations on the automobile and highway theme there was, of course, no necessity for theories on how persons would react to new public-transport services and facilities. The rapidly increasing demand for road space was apparent, highway construction funds were readily available, and public transport was seen to be, and indeed was, a declining industry.

In this context, the earliest travel models used by metropolitan-transport-planners attempted to predict the *usage* of public transport and of all modes in terms of the different characteristics of various areas (areas which in the jargon of the traffic engineer were known as zones, districts, and sectors). These characteristics summarised the social and economic circumstances in such terms as income, car-ownership, population density, and the like: the same characteristics which in fact were used to predict the *number* of journeys made in the city.

Since these rather unsophisticated models did not display features of the modes themselves they were unable to predict the response to changes in these mode features. More to the point, since the social and economic measures incorporated were generally increasing (car-ownership, income, etc.), and were inversely related to public-transport usage, the models suggested that public transport would be used by ever-decreasing numbers regardless of any attempts to improve the service provided. This was the situation in general terms when the concept of the North American urban transportation study was first introduced in Britain, and it was therefore out of step with circumstances where the overwhelming proportion of conurbation journeys was made by public transport and out of phase with the views and attitudes then germinating amongst those who determined transport policy.

The first step in this country towards anglicising the North American approach did little to change the situation in any fundamental sense. Some studies adopted the American practices without change or correction, while others carried out minor modifications which represented alterations in detail rather than in approach. These modifications were often the outcome of new attitudes to trip generation rather than the expression of concern that a distinct theory of mode choice was lacking at this time in the transport-planners' scenario of method. For example, the shift of emphasis in the analysis of travel generation away from the use of area data meant that public-transport travel was now predicted from data on the social and economic characteristics of the household or person undertaking the journey (Fig. 6).

Perhaps in one respect the modifications could be described as more than a matter of detail. This was the inclusion in the Leicester and London studies of a public-transport service or accessibility index intended to indicate the degree of service provided to each household so that the higher the index, the greater the number of journeys by public transport and the fewer by private vehicle (Fig. 7).

But in a policy context the index was of limited value. The measure used in the *London Traffic Survey* reflected the number of routes serving an area and the frequency of service. As such it could tell the planner little of the majority of options being actively canvassed at the policy level in the mid-1960's. It could give little or no indication of what would happen if the comparative speed of public transport was substantially increased by bus-priority schemes, or by investment in new railways such as London's Victoria tube line, or what would happen when the relative costs of public and private modes were changed by metered parking.

The Teesside Study attempted to modify the measure of public-transport accessibility to meet with some of these criticisms. The modified measures allowed for the relative times of travel by public transport so that the more accessible an area became, the higher the proportion travelling by public mode. Unfortunately, this unusual attempt to introduce a mode-split procedure distinct from estimates of travel generation, but before journeys had been distributed to their destinations, suffered a technical disadvantage which seriously limited its usefulness for policy purposes. The method assumed a uniform "service" in all directions from each area or zone, with the consequence that the modal split was limited in its

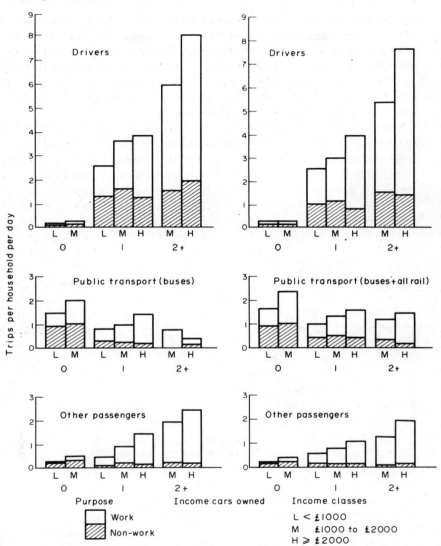

FIG. 6. Trip generation by mode and purpose for households with one employed resident in the West Midlands Transportation Study (left) and the London Traffic Survey.

sensitivity to the ease of movement along any particular route or in any particular direction.

It was not until the end of the decade that planning studies refined their procedures to an extent where the policy statements emphasising the role of public transport, made with monotonous regularity from 1965 onwards, could be translated into proposals and be subjected to systematic appraisal with any degree of confidence in the outcome.

The refinement that was needed was a proper explanation of model *choice*; the accent was now on the mechanisms of choice rather than in facile accounts of mode use. The new approach consisted of determining, *for those people who had a car available for use*, how they would divide themselves between using their cars and using public transport; people without access to cars were regarded as "captive" users of the bus and the train, for whom no possibility of choice arose. For those more fortunate, less restricted, travellers, the basic postulate was that they would choose

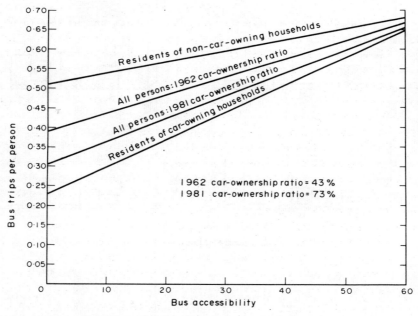

FIG. 7. Bus trip-generation rates related to bus accessibility in London.

according to the relative merits of each mode. In practice this meant·the relative travel times by the two competing modes, incorporating in the case of the Merseyside Study and the West Yorkshire Study time spent walking to or from bus stops and car parks. In this way the division of travellers by mode of travel was accomplished in two stages: an initial division into those with and without cars (often done as part of the travel-generation procedures because of its relevance to the frequency of trip-making) and subsequently, after journeys had been distributed to their respective destinations, a further split in the group with a car available.

In more rigorous approaches along these general lines developed in the SELNEC Study, the Strategic Study for the South-east, and the Third London Airport analysis the performance of competing modes was expressed as a "generalised cost". (By knowing the value placed upon travel time, time taken can be expressed as so many pence and added to expenditures on fares, petrol, parking-meter charges, etc., in order to work out which mode is cheaper overall.) In addition, where a difference in generalised cost between modes could be specified, the probability for an individual to choose one mode in preference to the other was calculated and incorporated into the analysis.

The mechanism involved in these later studies therefore was very similar and in some cases identical to that involved in measuring persons' decisions with respect to journey destinations as expressed in the "gravity" distribution model. In such cases a closely integrated trip distribution and modal split was developed, representing a further change of emphasis in the overall structure of the transportation-planning travel model. More importantly, it is a change which brings the overall structure of the model into closer accord with its philosophical base and a change which allows a choice to be made in a systematic manner between alternative policies which incorporate real options within public transport. Unfortunately most of the conurbation studies of the 1960's failed to make this change of emphasis or to make it early enough.

Distribution of Journeys

Representing the decision "where to go" by means of the distribution model has also seen substantial modification during the last decade. Earlier planning studies such as those in Leicester and Belfast used what was known as *growth-factor* methods. In a manner that was typical of a great deal of the earlier attempts at modelling travel, growth-factor methods were distinguished by a rather mechanical approach divorced from notions of how persons actually behave. In essence, the approach was a very simple one. It was to presume that the increase in the number of journeys by goods vehicle and by passenger· vehicle between any two travel zones would be proportional to the growth in the number of such trips generated in one area and attracted to the other. Such analysis, of course, ignored the costs and inconvenience of moving around. The emphasis was upon a change of scale rather than of direction, with the implication that as far as the pattern of movement was concerned, policy could only influence the situation by controlling activities and land uses. Manipulation of the transport system was inconsequential.

The fundamental and very necessary change was introduced for most person journeys, namely those wholly within the respective study areas, by a number of studies in the mid-1960's notable amongst which for their scale and importance were those in London and the West Midlands. Here the forecasted movements from area to area realistically assumed, "that as the facilities for road travel . . . improved over a period of years many people . . . take advantage of them by taking jobs further afield in distance terms than their present jobs".﹒ At the core of this new analysis, referred to as a "gravity model" because of the resemblance between the basic equation and Newton's Second Gravitation Law, was a mathematical function which described the effect of distance upon travel behaviour. The values of the function gave for different distances the relative probabilities of making journeys over that distance. The function is one which decreases as the cost of travel increases but its precise form or shape depends upon the way in which people perceive the cost of travel (Fig. 8). The London Study, for example (in contrast to the SELNEC Study), regarded a change in travel cost as having a bigger effect on behaviour when that change was proportionately larger.[8]

Although this kind of approach represented a very great improvement on what had gone before, "distance" in the London analysis and in most contemporaneous studies was measured in terms of travel time. Thus faster

[8] This difference between the London and SELNEC studies stems from the nature of the mathematical functions used. A description of equations based upon those used in the SELNEC study will be found in Appendix B.

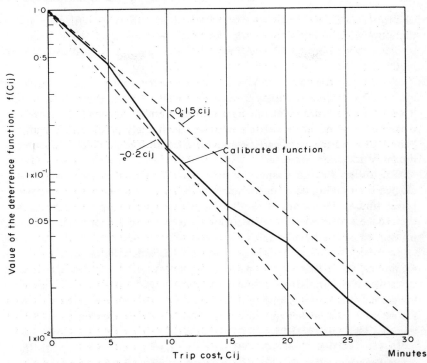

FIG. 8. A typical calibrated deterrence function plotted semi-logarithmically; this particular function relates to home-based non-work car trips (Good, 1971).

travel consequent upon an improved highway network or better public transport was allowed for, but the impossibility of measuring the effects of restraining traffic by parking charges remained.

A further problem was the emphasis in the earlier approaches on developing a separate distribution for each passenger mode. In the latter half of the decade the treatment of modal choice as a decision which depended upon the choice of journey destination required a concomitant change in the way the distribution of journeys was treated. It was no longer possible to distribute bus passengers separately from car-drivers because at the time of distribution it was not possible to distinguish completely between travellers in this way. It was possible, however, to distinguish between those with and those without the opportunity of using a car. In this way the distribution was divided and for those with a car and therefore with an effective choice of transport a "representative" measure of distance was required for the distribution model unrelated to any single mode.

The Merseyside Study responded by introducing into the distribution model the concept of journey time by an "ideal" vehicle, while the studies both within cities and at the regional scale at the end of the 1960's developed composite functions which had the effect of reducing the "cost" of travelling to a particular destination as the number of available modes of transport increased.

The other notable change in these later studies was to parallel the change then taking place in the analysis of modal choice. It was to extend travel time as a measure of the "distance" to which people responded in their choice of destination to include the other costs of travel which influenced people's behaviour.

In theory, these generalised cost measures provided the opportunity for examining the effects on the pattern of journeys of traffic-restraint measures which manipulated parking charges or charged directly for the use of congested streets. In a long-term context they also provided some scope for assessing the impact of those same policies on the disposition of land uses and associated activities.

In spite of their apparent sophistication, doubt must remain as to the effectiveness in practice of the later distribution models for assessing such situations. The SELNEC Study, for example, was unable to show the effect of parking charges on travellers' present choice of destination (although it was able to show its influence on the choice of mode). Their distribution model proved insensitive to such considerations and this led them to argue, in tones contradictory to the South-east Study, that in the distribution phase one is "modelling the decisions that people make about their relative residential and job locations and so it is quite reasonable to expect that they should perceive the spatial separation without considering costs precisely" (Wilson *et al.*, 1969). This may have some substance in connection with the journey to work, but for other journey purposes — shopping for example — it does not sound convincing.

From the mid-1960's onwards, then, the modelling of the overall pattern of passenger journeys improved progressively, and at a faster rate than the corresponding methods applied to freight movements. Whilst it remains true that the conurbation studies were beginning to make use of gravity models for the movement of goods, other studies in which the pattern of such movement was perhaps of greater significance failed to make the progress required for a proper examination of the proposals and policies under review. Of particular relevance here is the Portbury Study.

The problem was to appraise a scheme for the construction of a new dock at Portbury, Bristol. At the core of the appraisal was the need to estimate the quantity of traffic that would use the new dock. Freight for export originates throughout the country and flows out through the various harbours; with imports the process is reversed. The pattern of flow is the result of a large number of decisions by individual exporters and importers in choosing the ports through which to send individual consignments. A new port, or greatly enlarged port, will introduce a new option for exporters and importers, and will change the whole pattern of freight flows through the ports to and from different parts of the country. Thus the decision "where to send the freight" and the consequent distribution of freight journeys was central to the issue and at the core of the mathematical model used.

Statistics were available for 1964 describing the way in which exports from and imports to a given region divided themselves between ports. A series of general equations were set up which linked the flows of traffic through the ports to the amounts of traffic to and from the various regions of Great Britain and the distances of these regions from the ports. Distances, however, were measured in the model not in terms of travel time or the costs of moving and handling freight, but in mileages.[9] The consequence of this was that the forecasts in the Portbury Study of British trade in 1980 failed to and were unable to take account of the many changes in general accessibility which influenced the situation. There can be, as Mills (1971) has pointed out, changes for a variety of interacting reasons. There can be developments in shipping methods, such as containerisation, which would lead presumably to concentration of traffic on a small number of ports; developments in inland transport facilities; changes in the facilities, such as cargo-handling equipment and quay space, depth of water, and size of locks, available at the port in question and at rival ports; and changes in speed of turn-round and in charges in the port relative to other ports.[10]

[9] This was true also of the MOT's National Model; see I. G. Black (1971).

[10] A number of these factors can be viewed as the freight equivalent of parking charges and other terminal costs associated with passenger movements.

In the event, the predicted *pattern* of trade remained unchanged. All ports kept a constant share of growing national traffic; only the overall scale was altered, a situation which invoked Mills to remark that the Portbury Study's model "was irrelevant" to a proper examination of the proposal and thus a failure.

Assignment to Routes

Assignment of travel to precise routes in the transport system is an aspect of the models used in transport-planning which was the first to make use of computers and the aspect which has undergone the least change over the years in the fundamentals of the approach. The basic assumption involved in all studies carried out is that the traveller or shipper of freight will use the "best" route open to him and the best route may be the fastest or the cheapest or a combination of both. But whatever measure is decided upon, the important point is that the route used for a journey from one part of the city or region to another will be the one which affords the *minimum* travel time or the *minimum* travel cost, etc. The traveller therefore is expected to be fully informed of all the route opportunities available to him and to assess correctly the travel conditions upon each of these routes.

Any changes in method which did take place during the 1960's were within this framework of approach. There was a decided move away from the use of travel time alone towards the inclusion of the other costs which condition people's behaviour, particularly the out-of-pocket costs of running the vehicle or the fares paid to public-transport operators, and, in the SELNEC transport study, the costs of parking.

In the larger conurbations, developments included the separate assignment of public-transport users to the alternative services available for a journey from one part of the city to another. These comparatively expensive exercises took into account the frequency and timing of services (including the complications of increased boarding times as patronage builds up on a particular service) and the delays involved in interchanging between services.

Taken together, the use of generalised-cost and public-transport assignments permitted a wide variety of traffic restraints and public-transport promotions to be examined for their effect on the traveller's choice of route.[11]

The limitations that remain are due to the basic assumptions or, more precisely, the inconsistency between the basic assumptions of the route-assignment process and the assumptions made in other parts of the travel model. The nature of the process used for assignment of persons to highways and public-transport services presumes that people are fully informed of the costs that condition their choice of route. Prediction of choice of mode and choice of journey destination, in contrast to such "optimal" behaviour, accepts the probability of misjudgement; the different elements of the model are therefore inconsistent. It is to these broader issues concerning the structure of the overall travel model and the relationship between its parts that we now turn.

Paradigms

Although criticism has been levelled at the individual sub-models used during the last decade for the planning of transport facilities, what is equally, if not more, important is the way in which the various sub-models are linked to form an overall structure.

This overall structure we might refer to as the paradigm or "super model". It adopts a view of models that concentrates upon them as *systems* and therefore exploits them in terms of their connections, their overall logic, and their internal consistency.

The importance of the travel model paradigm stems from the ability to hypothesise a mode of behaviour by its internal ordering. Indeed, it is often necessary to interpret the hypotheses implicit in the sub-models, such as modal split, by reference to the positioning of this aspect in relation to the other building blocks of the paradigm. To pursue the example of modal split, the fundamental changes in theories of mode use over the last few years are to a large measure the outcome of the stage at which modal split was considered. It was stated earlier in the chapter that the *implicit* conceptual basis of the traditional or classic travel model is that the traveller first decides to undertake a journey, then proceeds to choose his mode, subsequently his destination, and lastly his precise route. Models in the late 1960's modified this sequence.

[11] They also allow for an improved calculation of operators' revenues and running costs and thus of changes in producers' surpluses.

The decision with respect to mode was now seen as the outcome of the relative benefits of modes for a specific journey; the comparison had to be made by reference not only to the location of journey origin but also to the traveller's destination. The decision regarding mode was therefore dependent upon the decision of "where to go". In the contemporary paradigm, then, the traditional sequence is modified so that the decision with respect to mode either follows or, as is the case of more recent studies, is made simultaneously with the choice of destination.

Of greater significance here is the use that has been made of linkages and connections within the paradigm to offset the inability of certain sub-models to put to the test some policies, particularly those concerning traffic restraint. The most recent approach along these lines has been to recycle (or iterate) the overall model until the resulting pattern of movements is compatible with that prescribed by policy. The recycling process feeds back the output of one part of the model sequence as an input into an earlier stage in that sequence. It is in this manner that overall consistency is achieved and indeed such an approach should be fundamental to any successful explanation of (complex) behaviour. But the caveat should be added that the linkages and connections should themselves be consistent with some underlying hypothesis of behaviour. It is at this point that the weakness of the actual paradigms used in some studies becomes apparent.

Good illustrations of this are provided by the Belfast and London studies. The Belfast paradigm is shown in Fig. 9. The salient points are the then unconventional, yet very proper, use of the household unit as a basis for the trip-generation analysis together with the use of traditional growth factor methods for distributing journeys from origin to destination. More significant is the structuring of the model by *mode*, with each modal sub-system developed quite independently of the other, and influenced only by a subsequent cross-reference to a process known as "modal-split assignment". In essence, modal split is made at the trip-generation stage and choice of mode is presumed to be uninfluenced by the relative performance of the respective vehicles. Thus the role of transport networks in determining travel behaviour is minimal. They have no fundamental influence on either the frequency or the direction or the means of travel. As a consequence, the capacity of the *basic* model for testing and examining policy matters such as traffic restraint and the promotion of public transport is severely limited. This was well recognized by the Belfast Planning Team and to overcome the

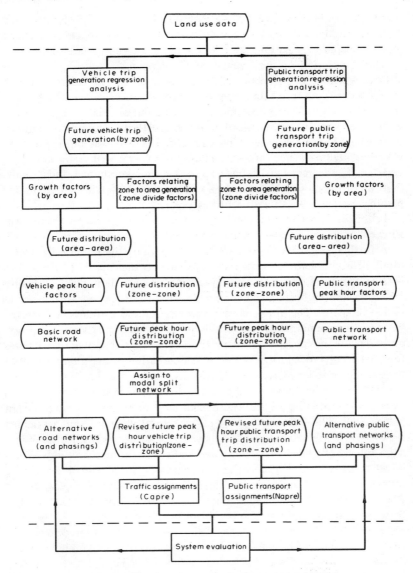

FIG. 9. The structure of the Belfast travel model.

Eidem in London)

problem a modifying process was introduced at the end of the model sequence, to assess how the basic demand for travel by private vehicle and public transport was restrained by the amount of parking space available.

The assumption of the "modal split assignment", as the process was known, was that diversion to public transport for central Belfast journeys would occur when travel time by private vehicles exceeded that by bus and train: a quite reasonable assumption to make, but one that evidently over-writes the assumptions made earlier in the travel model. In practice, policy operated through the cost of parking and this cost was represented by *manipulating* travel time on the private-vehicle network until journeys were diverted. The degree of diversion (restraint) was predetermined, and if on the first run of the model this level was not reached the travel times representing parking restraint were altered accordingly.

In this manner a particular policy, namely that of parking restraint, was allowed to influence the plan-making process.

A further example of such devices is afforded by the London Transport Study. The problem was essentially the same as that faced in Belfast. The basic model produced a severely overloaded road system which in reality would be limited by reduced trip-making and regulatory measures such as parking controls. The problem was to represent these restraints. The consultants to the planning authority chose to use a (linear programming) procedure to relate the capacity of the transport network to the apparent demands for travel. The procedure entailed the maximisation of the total number of trips attracted to an area, subject to the capacity of the road system in that area. The journeys restrained as a result of the poor capacity of the system were divided into two groups: those made by public transport and those not made at all. The latter group was calculated by assuming that restrained car-owning households behave as if they were non-car-owning, which implies a lower level of trip generation. Again like Belfast, the mechanisms were not based upon an examination of actual behaviour, a point made by Martin (1968), of the Greater London Council's Department of Highways and Transportation, who summed up the situation thus: "While this [maximising total number of trip attractions subject to link capacity] is a reasonable social objective it is not clear what policy decisions are required to achieve it. . . . Parking could be equated with the resulting trip ends but it is difficult to assess whether in reality the system would respond exactly as assumed by the model." (Page 8, footnote.)

Later Procedures

In spite of the misgivings about some of the earlier paradigms, by the end of the 1960's the more advanced studies had made definite steps towards building their paradigms with reference to the need for evaluations of the different plans. The travel models developed for the SELNEC Study and the South-east Study illustrate this point. The latter study represents also an interesting extension of the model-building concepts that were first applied to a large metropolitan area.

In contrast to the Belfast paradigm the South-east model attaches considerable importance at the beginning of the study to the role of the transport network, reflecting a basic understanding that travel behaviour is conditioned by the ease or difficulty of travelling about (Fig. 10). In this paradigm the network is seen to influence both the behaviour of travellers and the evaluation of alternative plans. Indeed, the calculation of changes in consumer's surplus now takes place in terms of those factors affecting behaviour. Consequently a crucial and early stage in the development of this form of model is to paint a complete picture of the network and to calculate the generalised cost of moving from one place to another.

The model is also structured by a classification of journey purpose, which reflects the new significance attached to the use of economic criteria for choosing between alternative proposals. The distinctions made in these studies between business trips, personal trips, and commercial-vehicle trips parallel the distinctions made between different values of time in the economic analyses.[12]

Implicit in this structure is the point that there exists little interrelationship between the journey purposes; the purpose of the journey does not alter as the travelling becomes easier.

Again unlike the earlier paradigms, the modal aspects are brought together and fully considered after the distribution of journeys to their respective destinations, thus presuming that the choice of mode is sensitive to the ease of movement.

---

[12] The recent North Staffordshire (Potteries) Transportation Study by comparison failed to make the required distinction. Classification was by mode, car-driver, car passenger, etc., and as such this ruled out the possibility of successfully appraising the different highway proposals in economic terms.

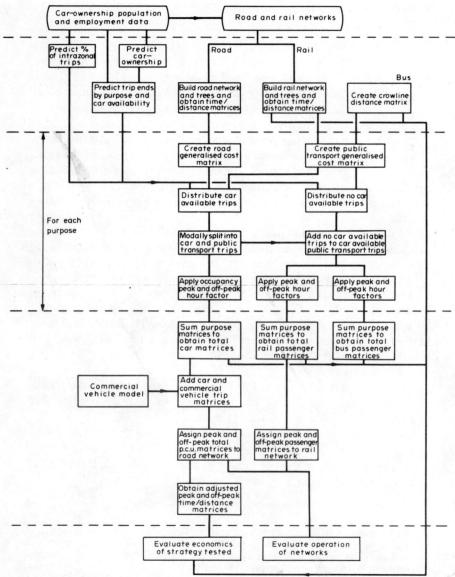

FIG. 10. Strategic planning study for the South-east: the structure of the travel model.

The SELNEC model is almost identical in essence to the South-east Study model (Fig. 11). Again there is the early emphasis on the network, the structuring by journey purpose, and the sensitivity of modal choice to the comparative performance of public transport and private car.

There is one important difference. The performance of the network is checked at the end of the SELNEC model procedure against the original estimate of speeds and costs. The model is re-run with the new data until a balance is achieved between initial assumed conditions on the network and final modelled conditions. In other words, the model is iterated to achieve internal consistency.

On this point the South-east team made a concession to the regional nature of their study. They argued that at the scale of the region, when the travel behaviour being modelled takes place over longer distance, choice of route, destination, etc. is less sensitive to travel conditions. As a consequence, an adjustment was made only for purposes of evaluation: the model was not re-run.

Nevertheless, in spite of these fundamental developments, the perfunctory consideration of goods movement remains. Both studies treated the commercial-vehicle aspects as an adjunct to the main model with the transport network playing no significant role. In marked contrast to their treatment of persons' travel, the studies appeared to consider that the pattern of movement of commodities could be predicted independently of the service provided by the transport system. A recent publication summarised the overall situation succinctly: "minimal analysis and forecasting work was undertaken, only enough to ensure that the total level of forecasted [commercial vehicle] traffic was correct". (Voorhees *et al.*, 1971.)

Such simplified treatment was perfectly adequate so long as the objectives sought were the improvement of the transport system in a technical sense. The peak period was crucial to measures of technical efficiency. But the movement of freight was of comparatively little importance during this period and those movements which did take place could be represented reasonably adequately by the methods then in use; the proportion of commercial-vehicle traffic did not warrant much attention, even allowing for the fact that the lorry was bigger and slower than the car. The use of economic objectives from the mid-1960's changed that situation. The peak hour was no longer pre-eminent as a problem and in any case in economic terms the importance of freight traffic cannot be judged by numbers

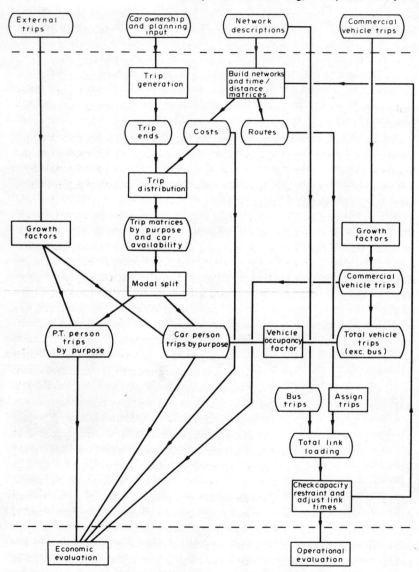

FIG. 11. The structure of the SELNEC travel model.

alone. The operating costs per vehicle mile (or per vehicle minute) of a heavy goods vehicle are about twice those of the private motor vehicle. The size, low speed, and poor acceleration mean that they impose considerable economic cost on other road-users. Similarly, the design specifications and maintenance costs of a road are heavily influenced by the volume of commercial traffic the road is likely to carry. All these factors make it essential that accurate estimates of freight movement are available for the economic appraisal of future transport investment.

A further criticism is that, in spite of their apparent sophistication and well-thought-out methodological base, neither the SELNEC model nor the South-east Study model overcome the crucial problem that trip-making is a function of accessibility. In this respect the basic paradigm again fails to meet the requirements of policy.

The one, but partial, exception to this failure was the paradigm used in the Third London Airport inquiry to forecast leisure trips by UK residents. In this instance the number of leisure journeys by air from any particular area of the country was modified by a measure of accessibility. The accessibility of an area was expressed in relation to the national average rather than in terms of total accessibility, but this average varied according to the system of airports that was being considered. If the new airport was further away from the centres of population than the original ones (Heathrow, Gatwick, and Luton), then on average the distance travelled to catch a plane would be greater. This was reflected in the accessibility index which in turn was used to modify the total number of air trips generated.

In spite of this limited compromise with the problem of accessibility (it was assumed that the number of business journeys and trips by foreign residents was the same for each airport system) the treatment of leisure journeys represented a most significant modification to the structure of the basic paradigm whereby the outputs from the distribution model were fed back as inputs into the trip generation model. The measure of average accessibility used to calculate trip generation required information, determined at the subsequent distribution stage, on the number of trips through each airport and, in the conventional way, the calculation of the number of trips through each airport depended upon the total number of trips made from different areas. This logical circularity was matched in the paradigm by a very necessary feedback facility, allowing the model to be iterated until the values for trips through each airport agreed at both the trip-generation and travel-distribution stages.

Of the travel models developed in the 1960's the surface-access model developed for the Roskill Commission was by far the best. Even if foreign and business journeys were treated superficially, at least part of the travel market was considered in a manner that was consistent with policy requirements. In this small way, the problem and the questions it posed were answered properly. Whether the prescription of the problem was the correct one is another matter.[13]

ICONIC SIMULATION: DEMONSTRATION PROJECTS

The development of a travel model has been the standard approach for predicting how persons will respond to alternative transport proposals. However, on the side-lines there have been one or two distinctly different methodologies which promise some measure of success in overcoming the cardinal weakness of the travel model.

Passing reference was made in a previous chapter to one such methodology used in transport-planning, albeit in a small way. This is the concept of large-scale experimentation, the testing of a proposal in a real world situation by way of a "demonstration", before beginning detailed design and implementation of the full system. In the case of this particular form of "modelling the system" the degree of abstraction from reality is, in a sense, minimal: the intention is to test the response to a proposal by observing how people do respond when faced with the rudiments of the scheme perhaps in a different location and at a greatly reduced scale of coverage or application. The methodological analogy or parallel is the "prototype" concept exemplified by the aero-space industry, or by exercises and manoeuvres in military planning. In systems jargon this basic methodology represents what is referred to as "iconic simulation".

The concept of the transport demonstration has been associated principally with testing and evaluating new technologies and systems of operation, particularly in the public-transport field. The rudiments of the methodology have been used, for example, in modelling personalised home-to-work express commuter services, such as those in Peoria and Deatur in the USA and the Stevenage New Town "Blue Arrow" service in Britain.

[13] *Op. cit.*, p. 13.

Nothing in its nature, however, prevents the demonstration from being used as a vehicle for testing a variety of new transport policies. A Working Group set up by the Ministry of Transport in January 1969, although exclusively concerned with passenger bus transport, did consider and recommend a series of demonstration projects which included the testing of changes in policy — traffic policy as well as schemes for alternative methods of operational control and for alternative types of bus operation (mini-buses penetrating pedestrian areas in Leeds, for example). Of the eleven schemes proposed by the Group in accordance with its terms of reference seven were concerned principally with changes in traffic policy incorporating various means of providing the bus with priority over other traffic.

The report of the Working Group nevertheless illustrates well the need for more thought to be given to the integration of methodology and policy in transport planning. The Group's terms of reference required them to recommend a series of demonstration projects. In this context it might be expected that the choice of appropriate projects and arrangements for monitoring projects would be conditioned by reference to a policy framework, in particular by reference to the alternatives to be examined and by reference to the manner in which the significance of the results was to be judged. As the Committee noted at one stage, "it will be necessary first to select the criteria to be used for evaluation". But the report provides little evidence that such factors had much influence on the choice of demonstration projects. A systematic reference to policy is provided only by a structuring of selected demonstrations according to the theme investigated — traffic policy, operational control, etc.

MARKET RESEARCH METHODS

An alternative but still comparatively little-used methodology is the application of market research/social survey methods for simulating the effects of alternatives. A very good example of the application of such methods is provided by *The Cambrian Coast Line* Study where the alternative courses of action were the retention of the existing rail service or complete or partial closure. To simulate the effects of the various degrees of closure, questionnaires were prepared to elicit answers from travellers about changes in the frequency of journeys, alternative means of transport, and alternative destinations if the rail service was not available. Thus, and this is the crucial point, the study based its estimates of travel behaviour in an alternative situation upon how people *thought* they would respond to what was still a hypothetical situation. Nevertheless, the study did attack directly the problem of how to measure the changing frequency with which journeys are made in response to changes in accessibility.

In this sense, the policy objective and criterion were clearly formulated (to measure the change in consumers' surplus) and the methodological design for testing the alternatives was closely related to the study purpose. Unfortunately, the "art" of this particular means of simulation, like that of iconic simulation, was in its infancy. Consequently, although attempts were made to consider how passengers would change their journey origins and destinations in the event of the rail line closing, the results were not particularly satisfactory and the analysis concentrated upon modal and trip-frequency changes.

PART TWO

The 1970's

CHAPTER 6

Reaction to the First-generation Transportation Studies

INTRODUCTION

It was quickly apparent that transport plans emerging from the transportation studies' computer models had miscalculated the popular mood of the time. Loop and spinal railways, a few electrification proposals,[1] and busways failed to divert attention from the very extensive "base-load" of highway schemes that the plans contained. Without doubt, the weight of recommended expenditure lay with roads — four-fifths of the total, for example, in both the SELNEC and Tyneside studies. Moreover, such proportions did not take account of the regular, but not insubstantial, expenditure on maintaining existing road infrastructure.

With such an unequal balance of expenditure and, bearing in mind the real nature of much of the analysis reviewed in the preceding chapter, it is arguable whether the transportation studies were not in essence cost-effective studies of spending £x million on highways to facilitate the movement of vehicles. Viewed in this way, many of the study analyses made sense, and some were extremely good. But, sadly, as we have seen, such excellent endeavour was misdirected and out of phase with public policy on transport, certainly from the mid-1960's onwards.[2]

---

[1] The Tyneside, Merseyside, and SELNEC plans all included proposals for new railways with an extension of electrification to other lines in the latter case.

[2] This is apparent if one compares the balance of expenditure proposed in the conurbation transportation studies with local authority expenditure in subsequent years. For example, Appendix C (page 130) illustrates that nearly half of the proposed 1975/6 expenditure in the metropolitan counties was on public transport, a situation altered little if one excludes Greater London.

COUNTER-PRESSURES

Not surprisingly, this incompatibility between the transportation study proposals and the public view led to conflict between the planner and the planned. The early manifestation of this conflict was the controversy over London's Ring Motorways, the highway proposals emerging from the London Transportation Study. These proposals were published by the GLC at the end of 1967 (GLC, 1967). The network proposed contained an inner ring around the centre; a middle ring on the line of the North and South Circular Roads, and the completion of Abercrombie's war-time D ring, parts of which had been kept as long-term objectives in various county development plans.

The ensuing debate, culminating in the Layfield Inquiry, is well known and documented,[3] but similar instances of strong *general* opposition to the highway emphasis of urban transport studies was to be found in many other towns and cities in the early 1970's. Moreover, the protest against motorways spilled over to suburban and rural areas, although here the level of debate was often more parochial and largely confined to those immediately and adversely affected.

Building upon this dissatisfaction, a number of organised pressure groups formed, re-formed, strengthened their membership, or developed coalitions.[4] The Transport Reform Group, for example, brought together in late 1971 members from the Council for the Preservation of Rural England and the Civic Trust, with the aim of determining research priorities necessary for a review of national transport policy. However, as the previous chapter suggests, it was not *necessarily* transport policy that was at fault, but the interpretation of it by the analysts in their models.

REFORM OF THE COMPENSATION CODE

Nevertheless, Central Government reacted to these pressures. First, noting at an early stage the developing opposition to urban motorway proposals, the Minister of Transport, after consultation with the Minister of Housing and Local Government, established in June 1969 a departmental committee to study urban motorways. The terms of reference of the

---

[3] See, for example, Thomson (1969).
[4] Details will be found in Kimber *et al.* (1974).

committee were to examine the policies then in operation for putting roads into urban areas; to consider what changes would bring about an improvement in the integration of roads and their surroundings, physically, environmentally, and socially; and to examine the consequences of such changes on issues of public policy, statutory powers, and administrative procedures.

The recommendations contained in the July 1972 Report of the Urban Motorways Committee, *New Roads in Towns*, drew upon the findings of extensive research by both the Urban Motorways Project Team and consultants. The Report, together with a full-scale review of the Compensation Code, formed the basis of a White Paper, *Development and Compensation* (Department of Environment, 1972b), presented to Parliament in October 1972. The resulting legislation, the Land Compensation Act 1973,[5] introduced a number of far-reaching reforms of the Compensation Code. These did not relate solely to roads or indeed to transport developments alone. All new public works used in the exercise of statutory powers were included, although highways and aerodromes were expected to constitute the real villains of the piece.

The provisions of the Act allowed for much-extended powers and for expenditure by authorities to mitigate nuisances from *new* airports, motorways, roads, etc. For example, under the regulations, authorities were required to insulate buildings against noise when the measured or anticipated traffic sound level exceeded 68 dBA for 10% of the period of time between 6 a.m. and midnight on any normal weekday.

If measures of this nature proved inadequate, the Act provided a statutory right to compensation for nuisance from the *use* of new public works, thus modifying a rule followed for over a century. The compensation was based upon assessed significant falls in the value of property caused by concomitant noise, fumes, smoke, vibration, and artificial lighting.[6]

In addition, there were changes in the assessment of compensation for compulsory purchase and the provision of a Home (and Farm) Loss Payment as a mark of recognition of the special hardship created by compulsory purchase procedures.[7]

[5] The Act does not apply to Northern Ireland: it was extended to Scotland by the Land Compensation (Scotland) Act 1973.

[6] The legislation did not recognise community severance or visual intrusion as a compensatable disamenity.

[7] Further details and commentary will be found in Moore (1974).

In brief, the new policy required transport developments to be planned in such a way as to minimise the disturbance and disruption they cause, and for any distress which remained to be alleviated by improvements in the Compensation Code.

REORGANISATION WITHIN THE DEPARTMENT OF THE ENVIRONMENT

A second reaction was for Central Government to reorganise its own administrative structures to avoid a repetition of past weaknesses. The formation of the Department of the Environment in November 1970, although basically a response to the long-standing criticism of the division of planning between Ministers, was undoubtedly assisted by the growing antagonism in the late 1960's towards motorway plans and their conflict with environmental quality. But, attributable more directly to the anti-motorway mood was the establishment, within the Department of the Environment in late 1971, of a group of planning directorates concerned with all aspects of urban policy, a move designed to curb, amongst other things, the organisational autonomy of the road-planning function (see Table 9).

The establishment of this group, under the general direction of the Department's Chief Planner and Deputy Secretary, Mr. Burns, profoundly altered the situation that, for much of the 1960's, had existed within the Transport Ministry (see page 19). The Urban Policy Directorate, for example, now combined under a single Under-Secretary divisions responsible for urban planning, urban motorways and transport policy, and conservation and amenity. This was in marked contrast to the structure of the MoT in the mid-1960's when the responsibility of one Under-Secretary was restricted to urban transport policy, a transport policy which failed to include even motorways.

PUBLIC CONSULTATION

A further reaction of Central Government was to confront and, to an extent, meet the argument that past experience called for more public participation to make sure the output of the computer-based models was "what the people wanted". In March 1973 the Department of the Environ-

TABLE 9. Department of the Environment Planning Directorates
(January 1972)

DEVELOPMENT PLAN SYSTEM DIRECTORATE

Division

Statutory Planning System
Statutory Planning Techniques
Planning Methodology
Cartographic Services

LAND-USE POLICY DIRECTORATE

Division

Land Compensation Policy
Land Commission
Development Control
Specialist Casework

URBAN PROJECT APPRAISAL DIRECTORATE

Divisions

Transportation Policy
Urban Roads
Urban Economists

URBAN POLICY DIRECTORATE

Divisions

Urban Development
Urban Planning
Urban Property
Urban Motorways
Urban Transport Policy
Urban Conservation
Urban Amenity

URBAN AND PASSENGER TRANSPORT DIRECTORATE

Divisions

Passenger Transport Industry and Investment
Passenger Transport Operations
Traffic and Parking

PLANNING INTELLIGENCE DIRECTORATE

ment and the Welsh Office issued a Consultation Paper which put forward proposals for a new procedure for informing people about practicable alternative routes for road projects and for obtaining their views about them.

Participation in Road Planning, issued in July 1973, analysed the results of the consultation and set out in detail the new arrangement for consulting the public at an early stage in the planning of *motorway* and *trunk road* schemes by the Department and Welsh Office. The focal point of the exercise was a public exhibition and the inviting of comments and preferences on the alternative routes described. In effect, the new arrangement added a number of *non*-statutory consultation steps preceding those required under the Highway Acts (see Fig. 12).

However, consultation procedures were neither obligatory nor binding for trunk roads and motorways. Nor were they a compulsory feature for local authority road schemes, although in the latter case authorities were asked "to bear in mind in developing their schemes the importance of giving the public early information about practicable alternatives and the chance to express their views about them".[8]

CONCLUSIONS

Of these responses by Central Government, the Land Compensation Act contained in many ways the more fundamental features. As one commentator remarked of the Consultants' reports and the Urban Motorway Committee's recommendations (and this point is equally true of the ensuing legislation), the effect was to make urban motorway building more effectively part of the wider planning process rather than a self-sufficient engineering exercise (Murphy, 1972).

This observation is interesting in so far as it suggests a tendency for transport planning to come part circle. It was suggested (page 14) that a basic feature of transportation planning in the 1960's was the distinctiveness it gave to the transport elements in the wider urban and regional system. In spite of the general reference to the applied procedures as "land

[8] As a further compromise the Government agreed early in 1975 (in response to parliamentary pressures) "that the need for a road scheme may be appropriately challenged at a public enquiry, providing that matters of policy are not called into question" (Expenditure Committee, 1975a).

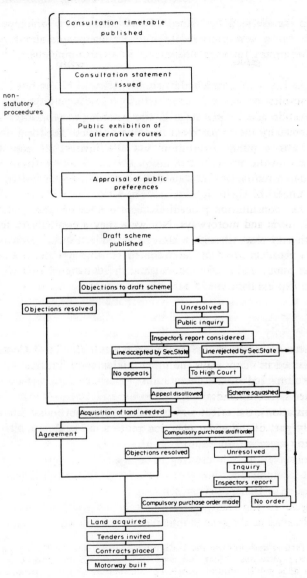

FIG. 12. A procedural obstacle course (a motorway proposal considered under the Highways Acts). *Note*: (i) Side-road orders are ignored. (ii) It is assumed that the Secretary of State is required to hold an inquiry in the case of unresolved objections to the draft line.

use/transportation planning", the role and treatment of land use in transportation studies was restricted to its influences on transport. The reciprocal effect was largely ignored except in a rather generalised descriptive way.

The position was summarised by the Department of the Environment in its 1972 evidence to the House of Commons Expenditure Committee. "Hitherto," they said, "transport studies have been used to test different transport plans within a single set of assumptions of land use: but not to test alternative land use plans. Where comparison between different land use and associated transport plans have been undertaken these have been only partial, covering their transport implications." (Expenditure Committee, 1972, p. 80.)

The 1973 Act did not of itself change this limitation in the transportation-study approach. On the other hand, it was indicative of an increased willingness to follow through some of the implications of transport plans in a wider planning context. Taken together with the reorganisation within the Department of the Environment and the designated role of transport policies in the preparation of Structure Plans in the mid-1970's (see page 103) the Act represented a more sympathetic and meaningful view of the relationship between land use and transport than had prevailed previously.

Consequently, a cynical view might be taken that the really significant contribution of studies in the 1960's was not to be found in their plans for new roads, airports, railways, and other artefacts, but in the pressures they brought to bear for a better integration of transport and land-use planning. Thus there is more than a tinge of irony attached to the Buchanan Report's expectations that "the mere act of preparing transportation plans would enforce the much needed integration of land use planning and traffic and transportation planning" (para. 449).

CHAPTER 7

Recent Policies

LOCAL-TRANSPORT POLICIES

The growing popular support for environmental lobbies (and their anti-motor-vehicle stance), the onset of the petroleum crisis in the autumn of 1973, and the subsequent down-turn in the economic climate strengthened further those trends in urban policy we have already noted as particular features of the late 1960's.

Following from the significant contribution to the general debate on transport matters made by the House of Commons Expenditure Committee in 1972, the Government of the day reaffirmed that its intention was "to limit the use of private cars for peak hour journeys to the centre of large towns and cities" (Department of Environment, 1973b). Once again, regulation of parking space and charging for it were seen as "the main means currently available to keep traffic within the capacity of the network and at a level which allows buses to offer a reliable service . . .".

Studies of alternative methods of restraint, such as supplementary licensing and pay-as-you-go metered motoring, "which some places may need in the longer term" (Department of Environment, 1973b), continued with the announcement in 1972 that the Department of the Environment was to carry out an extensive desk-study of a particular town, examining the full implications, cost-effectiveness, and methods of road-pricing. The GLC published its own exercise of a similar nature in 1974 (GLC, 1974).

Although it was also established policy for the Department to maintain a low profile in relation to local authority decisions — to encourage the adoption of certain policies but not to pressurise or coerce — nevertheless, there were indications that by 1975 the Department was willing to play a more positive role. A significant example in this regard was the refusal of the Secretary of State for the Environment to approve amendments to the

Development Plan for York providing for an Inner Ring Road on the grounds that "it is necessary to explore more deeply further measures of traffic management and restraint and the greater use of public transport" (Department of Environment, 1975a).

Complementing these attitudes were further, concomitant changes in the administrative and financial constraints having a bearing upon the local authorities' freedom of action. Particularly notable in this respect were the changes contained in the 1972 and 1974 Local Government Acts.

LOCAL GOVERNMENT REFORM

It is debatable whether the *ad hoc* committee structure of the earlier transportation studies, a great advance though it was, proved as effective as a single authority would have been in dealing with the transport needs of whole conurbations. The establishment of the GLC in 1965 was a first step towards reforming local government in a way more compatible with the requirements of modern transport planning.

A similar change for the rest of England and Wales awaited the implementation of the 1972 Local Government Act.

In 1966 the Government appointed Sir John Maud as Chairman of a Royal Commission on Local Government in England. A great deal of the evidence to the Commission stressed the importance of a system suitable in scale to encompass modern urban transport problems within the one level of local government and, in keeping with these sentiments, the majority recommendation of the Maud Commission was for a unitary system of local government.

The subsequent White Paper, Bill, and ensuing parliamentary debates resulted in some modification of the unitary concept and the system as enacted in 1972 established a two-tier system of 6 metropolitan counties and 47 "Shire" counties on the one hand and 36 metropolitan districts and 333 non-districts on the other.

In spite of the apparent dichotomy from April 1974 the radical legislation nonetheless focused the prime responsibility for highways, street parking, traffic management, and public-transport policy (and one may add the capacity for police enforcement) in the same hands: those of the new counties.[1]

---

[1] For Scotland a similar system was established in May 1975 as a consequence of the Local Government (Scotland) Act 1973.

Although the *ad hoc* PTA system was abolished the concept remained, and the appropriate committee (usually the Transport and Planning Committee) of the metropolitan counties took over the authorities' duties and responsibilities. The PTEs remained and two new ones were established within the boundaries of the South Yorkshire and West Yorkshire metropolitan counties. The boundaries of the existing English[2] PTEs were effectively extended or modified with the conferring of metropolitan county status on the respective conurbations.

The lower-tier district councils, on the other hand, in both metropolitan and non-metropolitan areas reserved the right to claim certain highway maintenance powers. "Shire" districts also had operational responsibilities for public transport and for control of off-street parking. But of greater consequence in the parking context was the placing of the general powers of development control in district hands. This gave lower-tier authorities control of private parking in commercial and other developments: a role not without significance in relation to traffic limitation policies. In view of this the Expenditure Committee in 1974 recommended reconsideration of the matter, suggesting that, in the circumstances, approval of the strategic transport authority of all matters concerning off-street parking might be appropriate.

also London Tpt Act 1969

PUBLIC TRANSPORT AND LOCAL GOVERNMENT

County responsibility for public-transport policies was established by Sections 202 and 203 of the Act of 1972. These required the County Councils, newly established by the Act, to develop policies promoting efficient and co-ordinated systems of public transport.[3] The Act also provided the local authorities with extended powers to support public transport financially and, subsequently, the 1974 Local Government Act (in contrast to the 1968 Transport Act) added financial incentives to the authorities' powers by allowing Central Government monies to be used in support of urban services.

[2] A PTA for Glasgow was established in 1973.
[3] In practice, however, there were limitations to the Council powers. The Traffic Commissioners, a body set up consequent upon the 1930 Road Traffic Act to administer licensing regulations relating to the bus industry, retained important powers. Notable was their control over the road service licence, a licence which, amongst other things, fixed the fare, type of service, and the route for every scheduled bus passenger service.

The omission from the 1968 Transport Act of Central Government subsidies for urban bus operations had been deliberate and not by default. The reason advanced at that time was that whether a local public-transport system operated at a loss or a profit depended upon local factors largely subject to control by the local community. "It follows that any subsidies which are to be given to meet operating losses of public transport ought to be provided by local communities." (Ministry of Transport, 1967b, para. 92.) They were able to do so by precepting the rates.

Subsequently, the post-1968 scheme came in for criticism. There were anomalies in the overall structure of what was a fairly complex series of grants and a degree of inconsistency in the way the overall structure was administered. For example, the Government was inclined to pay public-transport grants only when services were expected to be unprofitable (but socially desirable). Also, there were exceptions to the apparent principle of focusing upon capital rather than upon current expenditures, to wit, the social grants to loss-making railway services and the very considerable support to current road expenditure (maintenance) provided through the non-specific Rate Support Grant.

But the major criticism was that the grants, by concentrating upon infrastructure and excluding, for example, current costs of urban bus operations, biased transport-planning towards capital intensive solutions and was thus wasteful of resources.[4]

Eventually policy responded to parliamentary[5] and local pressures for Central Government support for bus operations, and it was announced in 1973 that bus-operating subsidies would be expressly included in the list of expenditures eligible for support in a reformed system of funding local transport. The stated intention was to "eliminate the bias towards capital or current expenditure or towards particular forms of expenditure" (Department of Environment, 1973c).

TRANSPORT POLICIES AND PROGRAMMES

The reformed system of funding was part of a much wider and fundamental change in the manner in which local government exercised its

[4] See particularly the evidence of C. D. Foster, Expenditure Committee, 1972, Vol. II, pp. 281–96.
[5] See particularly Expenditure Committee, 1972, para. 146.

transport-planning responsibilities. The most notable new feature was the introduction of a Corporate Plan approach reflected in Transport Policies and Programmes (TPPs) which each new county was expected to draw up on a regular annual basis and submit to the Department of the Environment.

The county TPP represented a comprehensive transport strategy bringing together policies and programmes of expenditure over the whole field of transport – public transport, roads, parking, traffic management, pedestrian and cycle facilities. Nevertheless, in spite of this transport focus, it was the Department's intention that the TPPs should relate to the town and country planners' County Structure Plan. Indeed, both the preparation of the TPP and the Structure Plan were to "be seen by the authority as part of a single planning process", with the Structure Plan setting the TPPs in a wider context and providing a statutory framework for publicity and public participation (Expenditure Committee, 1974, Q. 21).

The TPP was to include an outline of policies and objectives over a period of fifteen years or so, and a shorter-term five-year programme developing these policies, with the concomitant costs calculated in detail for the forthcoming twelve-month period. Each year this programme and the associated integrated resource budget was, so to speak, rolled forward.

To help in the preparation of the TPPs at an initial stage the Government gave broad guidance to each authority on the appropriate levels of expenditure for the five-year programme as a range. Counties were invited to present proposals for the five years in two forms, first as a base programme related to the lower end of the range and second as a preferred programme at a level chosen by the Council (Department of Environment, 1975b). In this way the important financial constraints that had been a significant feature of the transportation studies in the late 1960's (see page 17) were maintained.

Consistent with a corporate planning methodology the general approach focused upon objectives, and stress was placed upon a logical sequence of action in preparing the TPPs. Thus, counties were asked in early 1975 when preparing their second set of TPPs to pay particular regard to a programme clearly related to stated policy objectives arising directly from a critical appraisal of their transport problems, both current and foreseen (Department of Environment, 1975b).

Consistent also with the systems approach to modern transport plan-

ning, analysis was to play a significant role in the preparation of the TPPs.
Wherever possible, problems were to be expressed in quantitative terms so
that they could be properly assessed and progress towards them moni-
tored. Furthermore, in developing the arguments in the Policies and Programmes, conclusions drawn from a transportation study could be used in
support of the TPPs and, in a number of places, the Department of the
Environment specifically requested that this analytical approach be adopted (Expenditure Committee, 1974, Q. 44).

THE BLOCK AND SUPPLEMENTARY GRANT SYSTEM

Although the new procedure was itself a significant departure in many
respects from previous practice, perhaps of equal importance was the
revised manner by which Central Government grant aided the local authorities. Under the Local Government Act, 1974, most[6] of the Central
Government's *specific* grants for local authority purposes, which were paid
at varying rates to various bodies, were discontinued in favour of a block
grant system. From April 1975 part of the Central Government financial
aid to transport was included in an enlarged Rate Support Grant element
(previously only expenditure on road maintenance and improvements to
non-principal roads had been administered in this way).[7]

The remaining part of the overall budget was distributed through what
became known as the Transport Supplementary Grant (TSG). The TSG
was payable to counties whose *accepted* expenditure for a grant year
exceeded a prescribed threshold. In 1975/6, for example, the Supplementary Grant was payable at the rate of 70% on the above-threshold
amount (the threshold having been set to give each county £2.90 per head
of population, plus its 1974/5 expenditure on highway maintenance). This

---

[6] The new-bus grant was excluded. There were indications that the exclusion was
intended to secure the investment plans of manufacturers in regional development
areas. It was the Expenditure Committee's opinion in 1972 that such wider objectives
were not necessarily in accord with aims of transport policy.

[7] In new towns, to ensure that roads were built in time for development, a different arrangement applied. In each new town the development corporation took
over the main responsibility for the financing of all new town roads, but, by agreement, the costs were shared with the local authority in such a manner that over the
years the local authority would pay no more in total than it would have paid under
the old principal road grant system (Expenditure Committee, 1975b, Q. 2284).

is illustrated in Table 10, which shows the respective bids, acceptances, and thresholds.

The Supplementary Grant was intended initially as a transitional feature to ease the introduction of the new system in view of the unequal, but generally substantial, commitment of counties to schemes in the pipeline. In the case of the 1975/6 figures in Table 10 over 90% of the total was expenditure committed or unavoidable, and thus reflects itself in the apparently favourable treatment of metropolitan counties in the degree of above-threshold acceptance.

However, it is by no means certain that the absorption of the Supplementary element into the Rate Support Grant will occur or occur quickly. The TSG provides Central Government with an additional means of exerting pressures on the counties to bring them into line with national policies.

Under the new system Central Government policies are manifested either in the list of items of expenditure eligible for TSG or in advice on the level of expenditure acceptable under various items. The use of both approaches was to be seen in the Department Circular to local authorities briefing them in preparation for their 1976/7 submissions (Department of Environment, 1975b). Because subsidising car-parking ran counter to established policy of restraining urban peak-hour traffic, it was moved from the list of eligible items.[8] On the other hand, because of the need to reduce public expenditure, all counties were advised that improvements in highway maintenance standards would not be possible and that by 1976/7 revenue support to bus services would have to be reduced significantly.

In practice counties could ignore such national policy and undertake additional spending on unfavoured items. They could finance this spending from other sectors of their TPP, from non-transport spending, or by raising additional rate revenue. Specific Government approval is only required under present legislation in the case of capital expenditure projects above a certain size financed from loans (Department of Environment, 1974a). However, the present discretionary TSG could make an independent action by the counties a costly exercise. Retention of some supplementary element should at least strengthen the Government's hand when reviewing the TPPs, and this is an argument which the 1972 Expenditure Committee, for one, found persuasive.

[8] Items previously ineligible for expenditure included *inter alia* airfields, harbours, canals, dock facilities, most freight facilities, housing estate roads, toll bridges and tunnels, and new buses.

TABLE 10. The Transport Supplementary Grant 1975/6

County	Total bid at 1974 prices	Accepted expenditure 1975/6	% of bid accepted	Threshold level	% of total accepted	Expenditure above threshold	TSG contribution
ENGLAND							
Metropolitan Counties							
Greater London	296.03	206.28	70	84.45	41	121.83	85.28
Greater Manchester	78.06	42.85	55	24.85	58	18.00	12.60
Merseyside	44.36	29.79	67	14.68	49	15.11	10.58
South Yorkshire	34.88	22.57	65	13.26	59	9.31	6.52
Tyne and Wear	51.08	43.22	85	12.76	30	30.46	21.32
West Midlands	52.12	52.14	100	27.05	52	25.09	17.56
West Yorkshire	49.86	42.87	86	21.84	51	21.03	14.72
Total	606.39	439.72	73	198.89	45	240.83	168.58
Non-metropolitan counties							
Avon	18.24	10.15	56	8.41	83	1.74	1.22
Bedfordshire	15.29	8.07	53	5.00	62	3.07	2.15
Berkshire	17.42	11.77	68	7.30	62	4.47	3.13
Buckinghamshire	11.22	7.30	65	5.43	74	1.87	1.31
Cambridgeshire	21.29	7.88	37	5.97	76	1.91	1.34
Cheshire	27.93	17.34	62	8.84	51	8.50	5.95
Cleveland	17.61	13.96	79	5.52	40	8.44	5.91
Cornwall	8.31	4.63	56	4.39	95	0.24	0.17
Cumbria	8.78	6.68	76	6.19	93	0.49	0.34
Derbyshire	15.02	10.21	68	9.38	92	0.83	0.58
Devon	22.64	15.74	70	10.53	67	5.21	3.65
Dorset	18.32	7.03	38	5.73	82	1.30	0.91
Durham	9.25	7.10	77	6.07	85	1.03	0.72
East Sussex	13.24	8.87	67	6.54	74	2.33	1.63
Essex	22.10	15.99	72	13.38	84	2.61	1.83
Gloucestershire	8.04	5.75	72	3.94	69	1.81	1.27
Hampshire	33.86	24.84	73	12.80	52	12.04	8.43

Humberside	11.76	8.12	69	7.85	97	0.27	0.19
Isle of Wight	2.94	1.72	59	1.13	66	0.59	0.41
Kent	23.36	16.81	72	14.71	88	2.10	1.47
Lancashire	27.13	15.30	56	14.66	96	0.64	0.45
Leicestershire	10.33	8.58	83	7.52	88	1.06	0.74
Lincolnshire	7.61	7.62	100	6.75	89	0.87	0.61
Norfolk	10.23	7.80	76	6.70	86	1.10	0.77
Northamptonshire	23.18	11.88	51	5.67	48	6.21	4.35
Northumberland	7.26	6.28	87	4.55	72	1.73	1.21
North Yorkshire	12.85	10.23	80	9.33	91	0.90	0.63
Nottinghamshire	13.91	11.00	79	8.97	82	2.03	1.42
Oxfordshire	6.60	5.70	86	4.73	83	0.97	0.68
Shropshire	11.06	5.45	49	4.08	75	1.37	0.96
Somerset	7.25	5.01	69	4.47	89	0.54	0.38
Staffordshire	31.61	15.09	48	9.38	62	5.71	4.00
Suffolk	8.53	6.39	75	5.50	86	0.89	0.62
Surrey	15.92	11.31	71	10.02	89	1.29	0.90
Warwickshire	9.64	6.74	70	5.85	87	0.89	0.62
West Sussex	11.62	8.18	70	6.21	76	1.97	1.38
Wiltshire	9.75	7.41	76	4.75	64	2.66	1.86
Total	593.32	387.77	65	289.25	75	100.52	70.38
Total (England)	1199.71	827.48	69	488.14	59	341.36	238.95
WALES							
Clwyd	15.88	6.29	40	4.38	70	1.91	1.34
Dyfed	9.08	6.11	67	4.87	80	1.24	0.87
Gwent	12.18	7.69	63	4.85	63	2.84	1.99
Gwynedd	7.21	4.28	60	3.06	71	1.23	0.86
Mid-Glamorgan	12.00	6.74	56	4.83	72	1.91	1.34
Powys	9.96	3.69	37	2.68	73	1.01	0.71
South Glamorgan	15.58	6.20	40	3.69	60	2.51	1.76
West Glamorgan	9.16	6.35	69	3.25	51	3.10	2.17
Total (Wales)	91.05	47.36	52	31.57	67	15.79	11.05
Total (England and Wales)	1290.76	874.84	68	517.70	59	357.14	250.00

NON-LOCAL TRANSPORT

For non-local transport the same degree of comprehensiveness has still to emerge: there is as yet no equivalent approach based upon the notion of an integrated transport budget subjected to the transportation planning method. The prevailing philosophy appears to be that competitive forces should guide decisions in most sectors of non-local transport.

Principal amongst these sectors is inter-urban rail. By and large the judgement here is taken on a financial basis and, for national accounting purposes, the capital expenditure is shown usually in the Nationalised Industries Table of the annual Expenditure White Paper.

The chief exception to this approach is the capital (and current) expenditure on trunk roads and motorways which are the direct responsibility of the Secretary of State for the Environment. Because it is not possible to appraise road schemes as a revenue-earning investment different "planning" rules apply and the accounts appear in the Road and Transport Table of the White Paper.

However, in view of the circumstances faced by the railways, the logical basis of this approach is under pressure at the present time.

Under the 1968 Transport Act, measures were taken to place railway finances on a stable basis for the future. The loss-making freight sundries business was transferred to the National Freight Corporation (set up to integrate the road haulage interests of both the Transport Holding Company and the railways); grants were given for socially necessary but unremunerative services and for the elimination of surplus rail and signalling capacity; and there was a further reduction in the capital debt. After these changes the rest of the system and inter-urban rail in particular was expected to operate on a commercial basis.

Following the reforms of the 1968 Act, profits were earned in 1969 and 1970, but thereafter there were increasing overall losses. This was partly due to the Government's price restraint policy and the effect it had on holding down fares. In recognition of this, compensation was paid under the Transport (Grants) Act 1972. But the position became serious and the resulting cash shortfall could be made good only by borrowing at high interest rates. The consequence was that the Minister for Transport Industries instituted a review of railway policy. The results of this review were recommendations, provisionally agreed by the Conservative Government, adopted with some modification by the incoming Labour Government in 1974 and incorporated into the Railways Act of that year.

The 1974 Railways Act replaced the separate specific grants for loss-making services by a global subsidy for the whole passenger network. The network of services supported was to be specified by the Secretary of State. The Act transferred the costs of track and signalling from capital to revenue account to allow the value of such assets to be written-out of the balance sheet. In addition, relief was given for some pension liabilities and provision was made for grants to firms for the installation of private rail sidings.

In spite of the advantages rail freight obtained from this situation it, too, went into the red in 1975 and plans were made to pay an additional grant to cover these losses. The 1974 Expenditure Committee, reflecting upon this general situation, concluded that the overall approach to the appraisal of inter-urban transport investment was *ad hoc* and confused. Their solution was to have an integrated resource budget and to carry through some of the principles embodied in the TPP system for local transport. To accomplish this task they suggested an inter-urban planning Directorate within the Department of the Environment.

However, in mid-1975 the situation remained much as it was at the time of the Committee's report. Whether the implication of the 1974 Act and 1975 Grant, that the strictly commercial railway sector was fast disappearing, will lead to fundamental changes in railway planning remains to be seen. Meanwhile a transportation planning approach to non-local transport, based on a systematic and explicit appraisal of alternatives, remains largely confined at present to the road sector.

INTER-URBAN ROAD TRANSPORT POLICIES

Between 1957, when the Minister of Transport announced five major inter-urban road projects, and the end of 1973 road construction was very much a growth industry. Economic, administrative, and political factors all combined to focus this growth on inter-urban roads (and to frustrate intentions of devoting a growing part to urban roads). The White Paper *Public Expenditure to 1975–6* (Treasury, 1971) envisaged an average annual rate of growth of expenditure on new construction and improvements to motorways and trunk roads of 10·5% during the 1971/2–1975/6 period.

In June 1971 this expenditure was given new focus by the particular mention of six explicit objectives for the inter-urban road programme. These were:

(i) to achieve environmental improvements by diverting long-distance traffic, and particularly heavy goods vehicles, from a large number of towns and villages so as to relieve them of the noise, dirt, and danger which they suffer at present;

(ii) to complete by the early 1980's a comprehensive network of strategic trunk routes to promote economic growth;

(iii) to link the more remote and less prosperous regions with this new national network;

(iv) to ensure that every major city and town with a population of more than 250,000 will be directly connected to the strategic network and that all with a population of more than 80,000 will be within about 10 miles of it;

(v) to design the network so that it serves all major ports and airports, including the new Third London Airport; and

(vi) to relieve as many historic towns as possible of through trunk traffic.

The need to reduce the environmental impact of large lorries (the first objective) was a new factor of some importance in inter-urban road planning. This aspect took on profound political significance in a short period of time. While there was no explicit mention of the lorry in the 1969 Green Paper, on future road plans (Ministry of Transport, 1969a), by 1975 the policy was to concentrate resources "on the completion of a basic 3,000 mile network of routes designed particularly to respond to the use of heavy lorries" (Treasury, 1975).

Moreover, in the intervening period the Heavy Commercial Vehicles (Controls and Regulations) Act, popularly known as the Dykes Act after its parliamentary instigator, the MP for Harrow East, came into operation. One of the important effects of the Act was to require local authorities to designate for their areas a heavy-vehicle network.

Accompanying the revised objectives for the inter-urban programme were changed analytical methods centred around a computer-based discounting approach, known by the acronym COBA. This evaluation procedure, the development of which had been announced to the 1969 Estimates Committee (see page 59), was introduced as the standard approach in 1972. Most trunk road schemes costing over £1m and less than £10m were now appraised by this method. At the same time a completely new manual method using a tabular form of calculation taking account of environmental factors was introduced for smaller schemes (Department of Environment, 1974b).

The method offered "an improved means of determining the best alignment, standard of provision and timing of a scheme, as well as of showing the economic value of the scheme relative to others in the preparation pool". It was not used, however, to determine the overall size of the inter-urban roads programme: this aspect remained "a judgement by Ministers" (Expenditure Committee, 1972).

The factors behind such a judgement remain a matter for speculation but it is likely that the impetus and justification in political and economic terms for the overall size of the roads budget came from the rapid growth in car-ownership and general traffic during the late 1950's and 1960's. For example, the major review of the inter-urban programme in 1969 spoke of the need "to meet the rising tide of demand for road space" (Ministry of Transport, 1969a, para. 5).

Against a background of economic recession, slower growth in vehicle-ownership, and an actual decline in traffic in 1974, there were reductions during the mid-1970's in the inter-urban roads budget. The Public Expenditure White Paper of December 1973 cut back the average annual rate of growth in expenditure to 5·5%. But the most significant reduction was the revision of June 1974 which cut English motorway and trunk-road expenditure from a planned £248·5m in 1974/5 to £213m (at November 1973 prices). Although the Scottish and Welsh programmes remained largely intact for reasons of regional development, it was left to the subsequent Expenditure White Paper (Treasury, 1975) to underline the fact that, after nearly twenty years, inter-urban roads were "no longer a growth programme".

CHAPTER 8

Signs of the Seventies

INTRODUCTION

The genesis of transport policy lies in the way in which the transport problem is perceived. Although opinions differed, in one fundamental sense, for most of the post-war period and probably for longer, policy interpreted the urban problem very consistently. It was viewed as essentially a *traffic* problem that is a problem concerning the movement of vehicles. The journey-to-work problem, the problem of the peak hour, of accidents, of noise and fumes, are shades of the same complexion – the peak hour arises from the journey to work, and traffic congestion culminates in the peak hour.

There were times when the emphasis changed and these changes were often significant enough to require transport-planning methodology to change also: the old methods of analysis were no longer adequate for the new task required of them. An example was the change from the use of a technical criterion with its uncompromising emphasis on peak-hour traffic to the use of an economic criterion. Although at first, as pointed out in Chapter 4, this did not alter the situation as drastically as it might seem – essentially the same people's gains and losses were being measured – the later attempts of the Ministry of Transport to introduce equity aspects into the evaluation of travel time, together with certain other considerations, did have the effect of reducing the emphasis on the peak hour in what, nevertheless, remained a traffic problem.

In the considerable discussion about solutions amongst parliamentarians and others involved directly or tangentially in the formulation of policy, the references to traffic as the urban transport problem were unequivocal. Many of the speeches and reports quoted in previous chapters of this book make this quite clear. Of those with wider-ranging terms of reference, the now dog-eared Buchanan Report stems from "the study of the long-term problems of traffic in urban areas" while the more recent parliamentary investigation of urban transport planning was circumscribed by terms of reference which required a focus upon the journey-to-work. Appropriately, the Department of the Environment's chief witnesses in evidence to this Committee pronounced the main problem of urban transport to be precisely this, and the capacity of roads to cope with the problem (Expenditure Committee, 1972, Qs. 25 and 47).

Nevertheless, in spite of this consistency of emphasis over the years, transport-planning method has not been overtly successful at pacing the limited policy changes that did take place. To be forewarned is to be forearmed, and in conclusion therefore it might be profitable to reflect upon the current debate to see if there are likely to be further shifts of emphasis within the same scenario or whether, as one of the Select Committee witnesses claimed, "we are beginning to perceive transport problems rather differently".

PRESERVATION OF ENVIRONMENTAL QUALITY

A change of attitude is evident in the policies reviewed in the previous chapter. This change is an apparent willingness to give more emphasis to the environmental aspects of transport. If the real problem of transport is still viewed as a traffic problem, then we might argue that to some extent at least the nature of that problem has changed. The traffic problem is less a problem of congestion, frustrated mobility, and the like, but of the environmental impact and consequences of vehicular traffic and protecting society from its worst side-effects.

Such a viewpoint is, of course, by no means new. A number of individuals and interest groups have interpreted the problem thus for some considerable length of time — the 1963 Buchanan Report, for example, exhibited a sensitive awareness of this issue. But what is different is the adoption since the late 1960's of this viewpoint as a mass (though not necessarily majority) opinion and a greater willingness to make sacrifices in accordance with the view. With resources constrained by a low rate of economic growth there is some indication, manifest in the 1974 Control of Pollution Act, lower speed limits, etc., of a willingness to accept more expensive, restricted access in return for a pleasanter environment.

The Heavy Commercial Vehicles (Controls and Regulations) Act 1973 is a specific illustration of this willingness to curtail movement for environmental reasons. Under this legislation local authorities are required to publish, not later than 1 January 1977, draft traffic regulation orders for the use of roads in their area by heavy vehicles "so as to preserve or improve amenity" (Department of Environment, 1973d). In formulating such proposals Section 1(3) of the Act required consultation with *inter alia* "persons concerned with the preservation of amenities or the natural beauty of the countryside". Authorities are also given a new power to make traffic regulation orders "so as to deny access to premises by heavy commercial vehicles for up to 24 hours a day on grounds of amenity. . . . The Act is intended to achieve a proper balance between the requirements of amenity and the transport needs of commerce. . . . It underlines the Government's determination that lorries should be kept out of places where their presence cannot be accepted on environmental grounds" (Department of Environment, 1973d).

A PROBLEM OF ACCESSIBILITY RATHER THAN MOBILITY

There appears also to be an increasing appreciation that transport is really a means to an end and not an end in itself. Evidence to the 1972 Expenditure Committee drew attention to this aspect:

> Traditionally we have worried about problems of "congestion". Now we are more likely to worry about "accessibility provision". Deficiencies in congestion is a very crude indicator of transport problems while accessibility provision can be calculated for different types of people in different locations. . . . This measure also takes account of the spatial distribution of destinations which people are trying to reach. For example, one of the problems of people living near the centre of cities is that many jobs are decentralising, and so they are faced with an out commuting trip.

More recently, the self-styled Independent Commission on Transport in their Report *Changing Directions* (1974) have also emphasised the fact that the real goal is not ease of movement, but access to people and facilities. Movement is desired only to the extent that access requires it.[1]

[1] A recent policy study (Huckfield, 1975) has also emphasised the same point (see page 12). It went on to suggest that the relationship between transport and land-use planning should be re-examined so as to reduce the need for people to travel.

Defining the problem as a deficiency of access is not an entirely fresh way of perceiving transport problems. In a number of, albeit, restricted, circumstances policy has interpreted the problem in this or a similar respect for a number of years. For example, a belief was, and still is, prevalent that new transport infrastructure was required to promote industrial and commercial activity in the less-developed regions of Britain. Consequently, in certain cases the Ministry of Transport invested in roads which could not be justified if the perceived problem was one of congestion, etc. The Estimates Committee of 1969 noted that for development reasons roads with relatively low current traffic flows had been improved in preference to those in other areas with much higher existing traffic flows, and a Scottish Development Department witness appearing before this Committee stated that

> We take great account of fostering industrial development; it is difficult to say whether we take greater account of that or not. In some cases regional development has been the most important factor, as for example in the case of the M8 between Glasgow and Edinburgh. . . . In the case of the M8 . . . I think it fair to say that if we had stuck to traffic and accident loss calculations alone that road would not have been built for many years. (Q. 639.)

Similar factors were also evident in the different context of New Towns where the accessibility associated with new roads was also seen as a means of promoting industrial development (Expenditure Committee, 1975b, Qs. 2287–93).

What is new, perhaps, is the consideration of such accessibility issues in the more general context of local transport, as evident, for example, in the recent inquiry by the Expenditure Committee regarding the Redevelopment of London Docklands (Expenditure Committee, 1975c). Recognising the importance of access to employment, the Committee recommended that steps should be taken to secure the early provision of better bus and rail services and interchange facilities in order to improve access to employment.

Significantly, in reply the Government accepted "that early improvements to existing public transport services and the provision of better transport interchange facilities in and around Docklands are needed, to widen the effective labour catchment area for existing and prospective employers in Docklands and to offer Docklands residents a wider range of job opportunities both within and outside their local areas" (Department of Environment, 1975c, para. 23).

ACCESSIBILITY FOR WHOM?

Although there is an element of continuity and overlap on the issues of accessibility, another emergent interpretation of the transport problem places most emphasis on the question of an equitable distribution of access and mobility. These views find their apogee in the evidence to the Expenditure Committee by Hillman. Hillman, for example, sees the urban transport problem focused primarily neither upon the journey to work or accessibility to job opportunities, nor as a broader traffic problem as others have done. For him the main task is to enable those with difficulties in mobility — mothers with young children, elderly and disabled people — to get around more easily. The objective becomes one of minimising the discrepancies in personal mobility and thereby reducing the polarisation of opportunities provided by different travel methods. In this context current transport studies are seen to be based on the mistaken assumption that mobility and vehicle movement are synonymous; that everyone has or soon will have a car; and that the car meets the mobility needs of all household members. Hillman dismisses these assumptions and argues that the inequalities of mobility are growing.

> The present slight car-owning majority — in terms of households — becomes a small minority when individuals are considered: the number of individuals with exclusive use of a car is only about one-fifth of the total population. Projections of future car ownership show that even by the year 2000, half the population over the age of 5 will be without the optional use of a car. Even in households with cars, it cannot be assumed that the car meets the mobility needs of all household members. Though this assumption is often implicit in transportation planning practice, several studies throw considerable doubt on it. People in households live fairly independent lives although this varies with social class; the household acts as a unit for a relatively small number of journeys made by its members. (Expenditure Committee 1972, p. 237).

Again such considerations have not been entirely ignored in the formulation of transport policies in the past. For example, the 1966 White Paper *Public Transport and Traffic* pointed to the need to "provide for the large number of people — particularly many of the old, the young, the housewives, the poor — who will not have the use of cars" and more recently the Department of Environment have started a research programme "which focuses on the problems of access and mobility from the point of view of people rather than vehicles" (Department of Environment, 1975d). Such views reflect an increasing concern with the social aspects of transport-planning. To what extent public opinion as a whole will change further in this regard remains to be seen.

CONCLUSIONS

Thus, in these various ways, and in accordance with the paradigm of the planning environment sketched out in Chapter 1, the perceived transport problem appears to be changing. To an extent such changes follow from the closer integration, which the Department of Environment appears to be encouraging, of transport-planning within the Structure Planning exercise. This integration will naturally induce wider perspectives. In a recent letter to the Hereford and Worcester Council, for example, the Department expressed the hope that the policy section of the TPP submission might have regard to the wider planning, environment, and social objectives that are the concern of the Structure Plans and Local Plans.

But at the end of the day, regardless of whether these or other views prevail, if an analytical approach to transport-planning is to continue to play a major role in forming decisions, then a real difficulty lies in the political process deciding upon a revised criterion for choosing between alternative plans and proposals that is both generally acceptable and measurable.[2] When it comes to formulating strategies and policies there is this additional dimension to the problem — making explicit what is meant by a phrase such as "social objectives". And, as always, any fundamental developments in transport-planning analysis depend upon this essentially political decision. In essence, planning is a political process.

---

[2] Paradoxically, the initial response to the broader role of TPPs appears to be an increasing emphasis on "indicators" similar in style to and including the operational indicators such as "overload", average speeds, and the like, used in the earlier transport appraisals. If history repeats itself one may expect to see these indicators refined and given more direct economic significance in due course.

References

STATIONERY OFFICE PUBLICATIONS

COMMISSION ON THE THIRD LONDON AIRPORT (1971) *Report*, HMSO, London.

DEPARTMENT OF ENVIRONMENT (1972a) *New Roads in Towns*, Report of the Urban Motorways Committee, HMSO, London.

DEPARTMENT OF ENVIRONMENT (1972b) *Development and Compensation — Putting People First*, Cmnd. 5124, HMSO, London.

DEPARTMENT OF ENVIRONMENT (1973a) *Participation in Road Planning*, Department of Environment, London.

DEPARTMENT OF ENVIRONMENT (1973b) *Government Observations on the Second Report of the Expenditure Committee: Urban Transport Planning*, Cmnd. 5366, HMSO, London.

DEPARTMENT OF ENVIRONMENT (1973c) *Local Transport Grants*, Circular 104/73, HMSO, London.

DEPARTMENT OF ENVIRONMENT (1973d) *Heavy Lorries: Heavy Commercial Vehicles (Controls and Regulations) Act 1973*, Circular 128/73.

DEPARTMENT OF ENVIRONMENT (1974a) *Capital Programmes*, Circular 86/74, HMSO, London.

DEPARTMENT OF ENVIRONMENT (1974b) *Roads in England 1972–73*, HMSO, London.

DEPARTMENT OF ENVIRONMENT (1975a) *York Inner Ring Road — Decision announced*, Press Notice 91, Department of Environment, London.

DEPARTMENT OF ENVIRONMENT (1975b) *Transport Supplementary Grant Submission for 1976/77*, Circular 43/75, HMSO, London.

DEPARTMENT OF ENVIRONMENT (1975c) *Government Observations on the Fifth Report from Expenditure Committee: Redevelopment of the London Docklands*, Cmnd. 6193, HMSO, London.

DEPARTMENT OF ENVIRONMENT (1975d) *Annual Report 1974 Transport and Road Research Laboratory*, HMSO, London.

DEPARTMENT OF SCIENTIFIC AND INDUSTRIAL RESEARCH (1960) *Assessment of Priority for Road Improvements*, Road Research Technical Paper 48, HMSO, London.

DEPARTMENT OF SCIENTIFIC AND INDUSTRIAL RESEARCH (1960b) *The London–Birmingham Motorway: Traffic and Economics*, Road Research Technical Paper 46, HMSO, London.

ESTIMATES COMMITTEE (1969) *Motorways and Trunk Roads*, Sixth Report from Estimates Committee Session 1968–69, House of Commons Paper 475, HMSO, London.

EXPENDITURE COMMITTEE (1972a) *Urban Transport Planning*, Second Report from the Expenditure Committee, Session 1972–73, House of Commons Paper 57: I–III, HMSO, London.

EXPENDITURE COMMITTEE (1972b) *Relationship of Expenditure to Needs*, Eighth Report from the Expenditure Committee, Session 1971–72, House of Commons Paper 515, HMSO, London.

EXPENDITURE COMMITTEE (1974) *Public Expenditure on Transport*, First Report from the Expenditure Committee, Session 1974, House of Commons Paper 269, HMSO, London.

EXPENDITURE COMMITTEE (1975a) *Observations by the Department of the Environment on the First Report from the Expenditure Committee in Session 1974: Public Expenditure and Transport*, Fourth Special Report from the Expenditure Committee, Session 1974–75, House of Commons Paper 263, HMSO, London.

EXPENDITURE COMMITTEE (1975b) Minutes of Evidence, 2 July 1975.

EXPENDITURE COMMITTEE (1975c) *Redevelopment of the London Docklands*, Fifth Report from the Expenditure Committee, Session 1974–75, House of Commons Paper 348, HMSO, London.

MINISTRY OF TRANSPORT (1959) *The Report of the Committee on London Roads*, HMSO, London.

MINISTRY OF TRANSPORT (1963a) *Traffic in Towns: a study of the long term problems of traffic in urban areas*, Report of the Steering and Working Group, HMSO, London.

MINISTRY OF TRANSPORT (1963b) *Proposals for a Fixed Channel Link*, HMSO, London.

MINISTRY OF TRANSPORT (1964a) *Roads in England and Wales*, HMSO, London.

MINISTRY OF TRANSPORT (1964b) *Road Pricing: The Economic and Technical Possibilities*, HMSO, London.

MINISTRY OF TRANSPORT (1965) *Advisory Memorandum on Urban Traffic Engineering*, HMSO, London.

MINISTRY OF TRANSPORT (1966a) *Transport Policy*, Cmnd. 3057, HMSO, London.

MINISTRY OF TRANSPORT (1966b) *Roads in Urban Areas*, HMSO, London.

MINISTRY OF TRANSPORT (1966c) *Roads in England*, HMSO, London.

MINISTRY OF TRANSPORT (1966d) *Portbury: reasons for the Minister's decision not to authorise the construction of a new dock at Portbury, Bristol*, HMSO, London.

MINISTRY OF TRANSPORT (1967a) *Better Use of Town Roads*, HMSO, London.

MINISTRY OF TRANSPORT (1967b) *Public Transport and Traffic*, Cmnd. 3481, HMSO, London.

MINISTRY OF TRANSPORT (1968a) *Traffic and Transport Plans: Roads Circular 1/68*, HMSO, London.

MINISTRY OF TRANSPORT (1968b) *Traffic Prediction for Urban Roads*, HMSO, London.

MINISTRY OF TRANSPORT (1969a) *Roads for the Future: a new inter-urban plan*, HMSO, London.

MINISTRY OF TRANSPORT (1969b) *The Cambrian Coast Line*, HMSO, London.

MINISTRY OF TRANSPORT (1969c) *The Value of Time Savings in Transport*, Economic Planning Directorate Technical Note 3, Ministry of Transport, London.

MINISTRY OF TRANSPORT (1970a) *Report of a Study of Rail Links with Heathrow Airport*, HMSO, London.
MINISTRY OF TRANSPORT (1970b) *Transport Planning: The Men for the Job*; a report to the Minister of Transport by Lady Sharp, HMSO, London.
NATIONAL BOARD FOR PRICES AND INCOMES (1970) *London Transport Fares*, Cmnd. 4540, HMSO, London.
NATIONAL PORTS COUNCIL (1965) *Port Development: An Interim Plan*, HMSO, London.
TREASURY (1967) *Nationalised Industries: a review of economic and financial objectives*, Cmnd. 3437, HMSO, London.
TREASURY (1971) *Public Expenditure to 1975/76*, Cmnd. 4829, HMSO, London.
TREASURY (1975) *Public Expenditure to 1978/79*, Cmnd. 5879, HMSO, London.

OTHER PUBLICATIONS

BLACK, I. G. (1971) Some experience in modelling road freight plans, *Proceedings*, PTRC International Symposium on Freight Traffic Models, PTRC, London.
BORG, N. (1968) Transportation Studies: a review of results to date from typical areas — West Midlands conurbation, *Proceedings*, Transportation Engineering Conference, Institution of Civil Engineers, London.
BOYCE, D. E., DAY, N. D., and McDONALD, C. (1970) *Metropolitan Plan making an Analysis of Experience with the Preparation and Evaluation of Alternative Land Use and Transportation Plans*: Regional Science Research Institute, Philadelphia.
COLLINS, M. F. and PHAROAH, T. M. (1974) *Transport Organisation in a Great City: the case of London*, Allen & Unwin, London.
DOUGLAS, A. and LEWIS, R. (1971) *Trip Generation Techniques*, Printerhall, London.
DRAKE, J., YEADON, H. L., and EVANS, D. I. (1969) *Motorways*, Faber & Faber, London.
FOSTER, C. D. (1963) *The Transport Problem*, Blackie, London.
GOOD, G. E. (1971) A gravity distribution model, *Traffic Engineering and Control*, December.
GREATER LONDON COUNCIL (1967) *London's Roads — a Programme for Action*, Greater London Council, London.
GREATER LONDON COUNCIL (1974) *A Study in Supplementary Licensing*, Greater London Council, London.
GWILLIAM, K. M. (1974) Appraising urban transport policy — the new regime, *Proceedings*, PTRC, Summer Annual Meeting 1974, PTRC, London.
HARRISON, A. J. (1974) *The Economics of Transport Appraisal*, Croom Helm, London.
HOVELL, P. J., JONES, W. H., and MORAN, A. J. (1975) *The Management of Urban Public Transport: a marketing perspective*, Heath, Farnborough.
HUCKFIELD, L. (Chairman) (1975) *Transport Policy*, The Report of a Study Group, Socialist Commentary, London.
HUTCHINSON, B. G. (1974) *Principles of Urban Systems Planning*, Scripta, Washington.
INDEPENDENT COMMISSION ON TRANSPORT (1974) *Changing Directions*, Coronet, London.

JENKINS, G. (1959) *The Ministry of Transport and Civil Aviation*, Allen & Unwin, London.
KIMBER, R., RICHARDSON, J. J., and BROOKES, S. K. (1974) Transport Reform Movement, *Political Quarterly*, 45, 2, pp. 190–205.
KIRWAN, R. M. (1969) Economics and methodology in urban transport planning, in ORR, S. and CULLINGWORTH, J. B., *Regional and Urban Studies*, Allen & Unwin, London.
LANE, R., POWELL, T. J. and PRESTWOOD SMITH, P. (1971) *Analytical Transport Planning*, Duckworth, London.
MARTIN, B. V. (1968) Transportation Studies: a review of results to date from typical areas – London, *Proceedings*, Transportation Engineering Conference. Institute of Civil Engineers, London.
McKEAN, R. N. (1958) *Efficiency in Government Through Systems Analysis*, Wiley, New York.
MILLS, G. (1971) Investment planning for British ports, *Journal of Transport Economics and Policy*, 5, 2.
MOORE, V. (1974) *A Guide to the Land Compensation Act 1973* Estates Gazette, London.
MURPHY, C. (1972) New deal for motor way victims, *Official Architecture and Planning*, 35, 2.
OI, W. and SCHULDINER, P. (1962) *An Analysis of Urban Travel Demands*, North Western University Press, Evanston.
PAXTON, R. A. (1969) Traffic engineering and control before the motor vehicle, *Traffic Engineering and Control*, August.
PLOWDEN, W. (1971) *The Motor Car and Politics in Britain 1896–1970*, Bodley Head, London.
RHODES, G. (1972) *The New Government of London*, Weidenfeld & Nicolson, London.
SMITH, R. K. (1974) *Ad hoc Governments: Special-Purpose Transportation Authorities in Britain and the U.S.*, Sage Publications, London.
SPENCE, R. (1968) Transportation Studies: a critical assessment, *Proceedings*, Transportation Engineering Conference, Institution of Civil Engineers, London.
THOMAS, D. S. (1963) Birmingham's inner ring road – costs, savings and benefits, *Proceedings*, People and Cities Conference, British Roads Federation, London.
THOMSON, J. M. (1969) *Motorways in London*, Duckworth, London.
VOORHEES, A. M. *et al.* (1971) *Traffic in the Conurbations*, British Road Federation, London.
WILSON, A. G., HAWKINS, A. F., HILL, G. J., and WAGON, D. J. (1969) Calibrating and testing the SELNEC transport model, *Regional Studies*, 3, 338–50.
WRAITH, R. E. and LAMB, G. B. (1971) *Public Inquiries as an Instrument of Government*, Allen & Unwin, London.

Motor Vehicles in Use, 1946—74

	Year	Total vehicles	Cars	Year	Total vehicles	Cars
Sept.	1946	3,106,810	1,769,952	1961	9,965,300	5,978,500
	1947	3,515,444	1,943,602	1962	10,562,800	6,555,800
	1948	3,728,432	1,960,510	1963	11,446,200	7,375,000
	1949	4,107,652	2,130,793	1964	12,369,200	8,247,000
	1950	4,409,223	2,257,873	1965	12,939,800	8,916,600
	1951	4,677,888	2,380,343	1966	13,285,716	9,513,368
	1952	4,957,395	2,508,102	1967	14,096,000	10,302,900
	1953	5,340,222	2,761,654	1968	14,446,500	10,816,100
	1954	5,825,447	3,099,547	1969	13,751,900	11,227,900
	1955	6,465,433	3,525,858	1970	14,950,200	11,515,100
	1956	6,975,962	3,887,906	1971	15,434,400	12,580,600
	1957	7,483,489	4,186,631	1972	16,117,000	12,740,000
	1958	7,959,313	4,548,530	1973	17,014,000	13,521,000
	1959	8,661,980	4,965,774	1974	17,258,000	13,639,000
	1960	9,439,140	5,525,828			

APPENDIX B

Description of a Typical Transportation Planning Package (COMPACT)

The model is based directly on that used in the SELNEC study. The model is built for two modes of travel (car and public transport) and two person-types (car-owners and non-car-owners). Trips for up to six journey purposes may be dealt with in one run of the program. There is a choice of either a trip-end or trip-interchange modal split model. The main inputs required are network link descriptions for both modes of transport, and trip ends classified for each zone either by person-type or mode (depending on the modal split model preferred). These trip ends should be produced externally, e.g. by category analysis for which several programs exist (e.g. the STEP or SCOTCH packages). The distribution and modal split model parameters must also be input to the program. A range of values for these parameters should be tried, and the values producing the best fit with the existing survey data, for the base year of the study, selected (calibration procedure).

The outputs produced by COMPACT are:
- (i) minimum cost routings and costs between zone pairs;
- (ii) zone-to-zone trip matrices for each person-type and for each mode, for each journey purpose;
- (iii) the vehicle flow on each link of the highway and public transport networks.

The inputs and outputs are described more fully in sections below.

NETWORK BUILDING

The study area is divided into a set of zones. Trips made into and from the zone are assumed to be focused at the single point on the network (the "zone-centroid"). A node is any other point on the network, usually a road junction or public transport stop or interchange. These are used to provide more detail for the network link descriptions. Sections of the transport network are represented by links which connect pairs of zone-centroids and/or nodes. (The CDC 3300 version of COMPACT limits the number of nodes, including zone centroids, to 135, and the number of links to 540.) The link descriptions contain measures of spatial separation (conventionally these are distance and either speed or time) which are combined linearly to determine the generalised cost of a trip (along each link). This provides a much better representation of travel behaviour than time or distance alone. Thus:

$$C_{ij}^k = a_1 t_{ij}^k + a_2 w_{ij}^k + a_3^k d_{ij}^k + p_j^k \tag{1}$$

125

where C_{ij}^k = the "generalised cost" of travel from zone i to zone j by mode k,

$\quad\quad t_{ij}^k$ = the travelling time associated with such travel,

$\quad\quad w_{ij}^k$ = the excess (or waiting) time,

$\quad\quad d_{ij}^k$ = the distance,

$\quad\quad p_j^k$ = the terminal cost at the destination end of the trip (e.g. parking charges),

and a_1, a_2, and a_3 are constants that represent the value that the travelling public associates with each component.

After a calculation of the generalised cost of travel over each link of the network, COMPACT calculates the minimum journey costs between all pairs of zones and the associated routes through the network, using a fast algorithm.

DISTRIBUTION

In determining the number of trips between each pair of zones, COMPACT uses a "gravity" distribution model. The number of trips between each pair of zones depends on the number of trip productions at the origin zone, the number of trip attractions at the destination zone and an inverse function ("deterrence function") of the generalised cost of travel between them. This deterrence function may be either a negative exponential or an inverse power function. In general:

$$T_{ij} = A_i B_j O_i D_j f(C_{ij}) \tag{2}$$

where T_{ij} = the number of trips from zone i to zone j,

$\quad\quad O_i$ = the number of trip productions in zone i,

$\quad\quad D_j$ = the number of trip attractions in zone j,

$\quad\quad C_{ij}$ = the generalised cost of travel from zone i to zone j,

and A_i and B_j are defined to enable the trip-end constraints $\Sigma_j T_{ij} = O_i$ and $\Sigma_i T_{ij} = D_j$ to be satisfied.

Distribution may be either singly or doubly constrained. A singly constrained distribution is constrained so that the total number of trips originating from each zone exactly equals the number of production trip ends input to the model ($\Sigma_j T_{ij} = O_i$), but not so for the attraction trip ends (i.e. $B_j = 1$, for all j). For travel purposes such as shopping the attractions may be any exogenous measure of attraction (e.g. shop-floor space). However, in the case of journey-to-work the number of attractions (jobs) in each zone is fixed and we must use a doubly constrained model to make the total number of trips exactly equal the values input ($\Sigma_i T_{ij} = D_j$).

As stated previously, the user has the choice of either a trip-end or a trip-interchange modal split. In the former case distribution is performed separately for each mode and based on the zone-to-zone costs for that mode only [i.e. equation (2) is applied to each mode individually]. Within the trip-interchange modal split model distribution is by person-type. The trip productions O_i are subdivided into those by car-owner and those by non-car-owner. The trip attractions D_j are not subdivided as the two person-types compete for attraction opportunities. For example, for future journeys to work we can predict the total trips by each person-type in the production zone (home). The breakdown of trips by person-types at the attraction (work) zone will depend on the relative accessibilities of the zone by the two modes — that is, it will depend on the networks and will be predicted by the modal split model. The result of this is that equation (2) should be satisfied for both person-types simultaneously, for both demand the same values of B_j and D_j. As car-owners are assumed to have a choice of mode (i.e. car or public transport), the journey costs used in the distribution model reflect the costs by both modes.

MODAL SPLIT

For a trip-interchange modal split the trips by car-owner (for every pair of zones) are split between the two modes on the basis of their relative costs. The ratio of the number of car-owners travelling by car to the number travelling by public transport is fixed by the ratio of the deterrence function of the cost by car to the deterrence function of the cost by public transport. This deterrence function is of the same form as that used in the distribution model (i.e. either a negative exponential or an inverse power function), but may be calibrated separately with a different parameter. In general:

$$\frac{T_{ij}^1}{T_{ij}^2} = \frac{f(C_{ij}^1)}{f(C_{ij}^2 + \delta)}$$

where a superscript of 1 or 2 refers to mode 1 or 2, and δ is the "public transport handicap".

A second possible calibration parameter for the modal split model is the public-transport handicap (δ). This is a cost (either positive or negative) which is added to the cost of all public-transport trips in order to represent comfort, convenience, and any other factors not taken into account in the generalised cost formula. It must be noted, however, that (as in the SELNEC model) this cost is included only in the modal split model and is ignored for the purposes of distribution.

ASSIGNMENT

All trips between each zone pair, and by each mode, are allocated to the minimum cost path defined during the network building process (all-or-nothing assignment). The total trips on any link of the network are equivalent to the flow or load. There is no capacity restraint procedure in COMPACT, so should these flows be unrealistically high compared with the initial assumptions used in determining the speed on the links, then it may be necessary to re-run the program with corrected speed values.

INPUTS

A run of COMPACT requires the following inputs:

(i) *Option Control Cards*. These contain the title of the run, and details of the number of zones, nodes, journey purposes, etc., required. They also define the form of the model (e.g. the type of distribution and modal split models) and the amount of printed output required.

(ii) *Cost Parameter Cards*. These define the parameters to be used in the generalised cost formula. These are defined for each link classification (see below) in both highway and public-transport networks.

(iii) *Link Cards*. Each link of both networks must be defined by a card which specifies:

(a) a classification number (or "jurisdiction code") which determines the set of generalised cost parameters that should be used for this link. This is used mainly to distinguish between walking and waiting, and bus and train, links.

(b) Node A. The identification number of the node or zone centroid at the start of this link. Zone centroids and nodes are numbered consecutively.

(c) Node B. The number of the node or centroid at the end of this link. All links may be defined as two-way in which case Node A and Node B are interchangeable and the link has the same characteristics in both directions. Alternatively, on the option control cards, the links may be defined as one-way, in which case the link may be travelled only in the direction from A to B; in this case a two-way road in the network must be defined as two links.

(d) The length of the link, in convenient units.

(e) An indicator as to whether the next value (f) is a speed or time.

(f) Depending on (e), either the speed [in units compatible with those of (d)] of travel over the link or the time taken to traverse it.

(iv) *Intrazonal Costs*. The generalised cost, by each mode, associated with an intrazonal trip (i.e. a trip that originates and terminates within a zone), must be input for each zone. Zoning systems are usually designed to minimise the number of these trips, for not only are these costs difficult to estimate, but it is also not usually possible to assign these trips to the transport networks.

(v) *Terminal Costs*. As stated earlier, all trips originating or terminating within each zone are assumed to do so at a single point on the networks. It is often necessary to include a cost which represents the average cost of travelling from individual points in a zone to the zone centroid. Therefore, for each zone and for each mode, one must specify this access or terminal cost -- first for trips originating in each zone, and then for trips terminating in each zone. The latter set of costs may also be used to include parking charges [the p_j^k term in equation (1)].

(vi) *Trip Ends*. For each zone the number of trips originating and terminating, subdivided either by person-type or mode, must be specified.

(vii) *Distribution and Modal Split Parameters*. These parameters control the form and "shape" of the deterrence function used in the distribution and modal split processes. Having used existing survey data to produce appropriate values (calibration), these same values are used for all future runs.

OUTPUTS

The line-printer outputs from a run of COMPACT are:

(i) A copy of the option control cards for checking.

(ii) For each network in turn the values on the cost parameter cards and the number of links in the network, followed by a sorted list of links containing the Node A, the Node B, the classification (or Jurisdiction code), the distance, and the time (calculated from the speed if necessary) for each link.

(iii) Also for each network a matrix of "back-nodes" is printed. These indicate the penultimate node (or zone) on the minimum cost path between a pair of zones or nodes. From these the complete minimum cost paths between pairs of zones can easily be traced.

(iv) A copy of intrazonal and terminal costs for checking.

(v) Matrices of zone-to-zone costs indicating the total cost, in generalised cost units, by each mode of travel between every pair of zones.

(vi) A copy of the input trip ends, and distribution and modal split parameters.

(vii) Trip matrices indicating the number of person-trips (and/or vehicle trips) by each mode and/or person-type, between every pair of zones.

(viii) A list indicating the vehicle loading on each link of each network. The list shows the Node A, the Node B, and the vehicle loading or assignment.

AVAILABILITY

COMPACT II, the CDC 3300 version of COMPACT, was made generally available to local authorities, consultants, and other interested parties by the Department of the Environment in April 1971. Several prospective users have converted COMPACT to their own machines and versions now exist for the CDC 6600, ICL 1900 series, IBM 360 series and Univac computers.

APPENDIX C

Transport Policies and Programmes 1975/6
(£ million November 1973 prices)

	Highways					Public Transport			Other expenditure	Total TPP 1975/6	Total TPP 1974/5	% change
	Constr. and land	Mainte-nance	Lighting	Other	Total	Capital	Current	Total				
Metropolitan Counties												
Greater London	48.20	40.29	7.35	6.82	102.66	Rail 33.06 / Other 12.44	Rail 15.00 / Other 55.35	115.85	10.97	229.48	132.14	+74
Greater Manchester	13.97	8.90	3.30	1.40	27.57	Rail 14.44 / Other 3.70	Rail 5.20 / Other 5.85	29.19	3.75	60.51	39.10	+55
Merseyside	7.75	5.65	2.12	2.44	17.96	Rail 9.49 / Other 0.79	Rail – / Other 4.71	14.99	1.44	34.39	25.34	+36
South Yorkshire	8.36	9.15	1.30	–	18.81	Rail 0.05 / Other 1.88	Rail 0.35 / Other 4.98	7.26	0.97	27.04	18.74	+44
Tyne and Wear	14.39	5.00	2.33	–	21.72	Rail 20.03 / Other 1.29	Rail 1.70 / Other 1.03	24.05	2.34	48.11	28.18	+17
West Midlands	14.29	9.74	2.53	–	26.56	Rail 2.35 / Other 0.35	Rail 3.30 / Other 6.02	12.02	1.82	40.40	40.83	–1
West Yorkshire	14.66	9.15	2.62	2.99	29.42	Rail 0.20 / Other 2.57	Rail 0.80 / Other 4.54	8.11	1.12	38.65	33.56	+15
Total	121.62	87.88	21.55	13.65	244.70	102.64	108.83	211.47	22.41	478.58	317.89	+51
Non-Metropolitan Counties												
Avon	7.16	4.08	0.78	0.32	12.34	0.02	0.18	0.20	1.59	14.14	...	...
Bedfordshire	6.12	2.26	0.37	0.03	8.78	0.50	0.30	0.80	2.27	11.85	10.50	+13
Berkshire	7.43	3.64	0.59	0.09	11.75	0.22	0.19	0.41	1.34	13.50	11.85	+14
Buckinghamshire	5.00	2.53	0.33	0.33	8.19	0.10	0.28	0.38	0.13	8.70	8.14	+7
Cambridgeshire	11.24	3.03	0.52	0.26	15.05	0.31	0.13	0.44	1.01	16.50	13.16	+25
Cheshire	12.78	5.50	0.75	0.11	19.14	1.06	0.56	1.62	0.89	21.65	14.75	+47
Cleveland	9.31	1.87	0.71	0.73	12.62	0.26	0.02	0.28	0.75	13.65	10.16	+34
Cornwall	2.32	2.52	0.25	0.18	5.27	–	0.07	0.07	1.10	6.44	3.91	+65
Cumbria	1.54	3.84	...	...	5.89	–	0.15	0.15	0.77	6.81	6.67	+2
Derbyshire	5.41	4.10	0.96	0.35	10.82	0.12	0.37	0.49	0.33	11.64	9.01	+29
Devon	9.13	5.38	0.76	0.40	15.67	0.44	0.39	0.83	4.85	21.35	17.36	+23
Dorset	9.31	2.92	0.64	0.13	13.00	0.13	0.38	0.51	0.69	14.20	9.94	+43

County												
Essex	6.79	6.69	1.24	0.71	15.44	0.10	0.58	0.68	1.01	17.13	12.33	+39
Gloucestershire	3.43	1.83	0.24	0.28	5.78	0.06	0.16	0.22	0.23	6.23	4.86	+28
Hampshire	16.36	5.32	0.92	0.08	22.68	0.91	0.55	1.46	2.11	26.25	23.62	+11
Hereford and Worcs.	11.26	4.08	0.56	0.23	16.13	0.73	0.14	0.87	0.35	17.35	11.27	+54
Hertfordshire	6.38	5.80	0.98	–	13.16	–	0.80	0.80	1.44	15.40	11.23	+26
Humberside	2.93	4.94	0.20	0.75	8.82	0.39	0.08	0.08	0.22	9.12	6.48	+41
Isle of Wight	0.78	0.73	0.13	0.13	1.77	0.48	0.05	0.08	0.07	2.28	1.68	+36
Kent	8.20	6.76	1.05	0.46	16.47	1.06	0.31	0.44	0.85	18.11	14.61	+24
Lancashire	8.51	7.22	1.77	–	17.50	1.06	0.20	1.26	2.27	21.03	13.84	+52
Leicestershire	2.84	3.63	0.82	0.21	7.50	0.08	0.35	0.43	0.08	8.01	6.40	+25
Lincolnshire	1.38	4.01	0.20	–	5.59	0.08	0.10	0.12	0.19	5.90	5.51	+7
Norfolk	3.42	2.85	0.50	0.36	7.13	0.02	0.22	0.22	0.58	7.93	6.82	+16
Northamptonshire	11.08	2.65	0.34	0.91	14.98	0.77	0.43	1.20	1.79	17.97	14.58	+23
Northumberland	2.39	2.76	...	0.70	5.04	0.05	0.15	0.20	0.39	5.63	5.08	+11
North Yorkshire	2.41	5.85	0.47	0.25	9.43	–	0.12	0.12	0.41	9.96	9.06	+10
Nottinghamshire	4.92	4.02	0.30	0.25	9.49	0.27	0.77	1.04	0.25	10.78	9.21	+17
Oxfordshire	1.73	2.02	0.38	0.26	4.39	0.15	0.43	0.58	0.46	5.12	5.21	–2
Shropshire	5.33	2.35	0.20	0.08	7.96	0.15	0.15	0.15	0.46	8.57	5.05	+70
Somerset	3.09	2.19	0.19	0.06	5.53	–	0.06	0.06	0.03	5.62	5.20	+8
Staffordshire	...	...	...	...	...	...	...	...	...	...	24.50	...
Suffolk	2.59	2.45	0.28	0.01	5.33	0.04	0.43	0.47	0.81	6.61	5.84	+13
Surrey	6.19	4.35	0.74	–	11.28	0.02	0.46	0.48	0.58	12.34	9.54	+29
Warwickshire	2.82	3.88	0.36	0.04	7.10	0.01	0.15	0.16	0.21	7.47	5.79	+29
West Sussex	4.43	2.72	0.38	0.39	7.92	–	0.43	0.43	0.66	9.01	6.95	+30
Wiltshire	3.61	2.27	0.23	0.07	6.18	0.29	0.14	0.43	0.95	7.56	7.75	–2
Total					387.07*			19.55*	32.61*	463.74	337.79†	+26†
Total (England)					631.77*			231.02*	55.02*	942.32	655.68†	+38†
Welsh Counties												
Clwyd	7.93	2.61	0.41	0.20	11.15	0.20	0.44	0.64	0.52	12.31	7.51	+64
Dyfed	2.74	3.23	0.35	0.19	6.51	0.08	0.29	0.37	0.16	7.04	5.79	+22
Gwent	5.60	2.72	0.25	0.27	8.84	0.07	0.34	0.41	0.19	9.44	8.95	+5
Gwynedd	2.61	1.98	0.20	0.23	5.02	0.06	0.21	0.27	0.30	5.59	4.78	+17
Mid Glamorgan	5.13	2.60	0.66	–	8.39	0.30	0.35	0.65	0.26	9.30	6.80	+37
Powys	3.68	3.57	0.10	0.05	7.40	0.06	0.08	0.14	0.18	7.72	4.95	+56
South Glamorgan	...	1.98	...	0.44	10.46	0.88	0.52	1.40	0.22	12.08	7.78	+55
West Glamorgan	3.72	1.80	0.41	0.44	6.37	0.12	0.45	0.57	0.16	7.10	6.00	+18
Total (Wales)					64.14			4.45	1.99	70.58	52.56	+34
Total (England and Wales)					695.91*			235.47*	57.01*	1,012.90	708.24†	+38

– Nil.   ... Not available.   * Excluding Staffordshire.   † Excluding Staffordshire and Avon.

APPENDIX D

Public Expenditure and Transport
£ million at 1974 survey prices. Treasury (1975)

	Actual						Forecast			
	1969-70	1970-1	1971-2	1972-3	1973-4	1974-5	1975-6	1976-7	1977-8	1978-9
Motorways and trunk roads										
New construction and improvement	300.4	364.8	312.4	286.7	324.2	315.9	319.9	334.1	349	359
Maintenance	29.5	33.5	38.0	52.5	60.2	42.3	50.5	51.6	56	59
Total	329.9	398.3	350.4	339.2	384.4	358.2	370.4	385.7	405	418
Local transport										
Capital										
Investment by local transport authorities										
Roads – new construction and improvement	287.2	341.0	347.4	335.1	370.7	309.4	277.6	279.9	276	276
Car parks	19.4	29.8	22.6	20.4	17.5	21.7	24.7	25.3	26	28
Public transport investment	33.9	52.4	50.7	90.6	81.8	95.2	103.4	110.8	112	114
Current										
Roads – maintenance	262.0	259.6	280.0	287.4	286.9	284.5	285.4	294.2	304	310
Car parks	– 3.9	– 6.0	– 5.0	– 5.7	– 6.4	– 6.2	– 9.2	– 12.8	– 18	– 21
Other expenditure	1.8	3.1	3.3	4.4	5.7	6.0	6.0	6.8	8	8
Local authority administration	62.7	66.7	69.1	68.5	74.6	92.5	92.4	95.9	100	104
Passenger transport subsidies										
British Rail	–	–	–	11.6	10.9	15.6	19.5	20.1	21	21
Other	1.6	2.9	4.3	5.9	15.3	95.5	111.5	96.3	81	66
Total	664.7	749.5	772.4	818.?	857.0	914.?	911.3	916.5	910	906

British Rail	119.2	92.8	92.7	113.7	181.1	275.2	297.7	314.2	322	343
British Waterways Board	2.8	3.7	4.5	4.9	5.4	5.6	5.7	5.7	6	6
National Freight Corporation	25.9	17.5	10.2	4.0	1.7	–	–	–	–	–
London Transport Board	16.3	2.5	–	–	–	–	–	–	–	–
Scottish Transport Group	0.6	0.8	0.5	0.8	0.8	0.6	0.4	0.4	–	1
National Bus Company	–	–	0.4	8.2	–	–	–	–	–	–
Other										
Bus fuel grants	31.1	29.9	27.2	24.4	20.3	39.0	31.7	27.9	27	32
New bus grants to private operators	0.3	0.3	0.8	3.2	3.4	3.0	3.0	3.0	3	3
Other Central Government subsidies	0.6	0.3	0.3	0.2	0.4	1.4	3.3	3.1	3	3
Total	196.8	147.8	136.6	159.4	213.1	324.8	341.8	354.3	361	379
Ports and shipping										
Ports	52.6	40.9	39.2	52.1	32.6	32.9	40.8	41.2	48	45
Shipping	2.5	4.9	4.6	4.2	5.3	5.9	6.2	6.2	6	6
Total	55.1	45.8	43.8	56.3	37.9	38.8	47.0	47.4	54	51
British Airways Board	89.5	141.9	130.2	58.1	83.4	106.1	144.0	103.1	98	103
British Airports Authority	16.0	13.5	15.1	15.9	21.0	22.6	36.5	30.8	27	25
Total airways and airports	105.5	155.4	145.3	74.0	104.4	128.7	180.5	133.9	125	128
British Railway Board	131.9	133.6	111.6	131.1	142.8	143.2	197.4	232.7	247	247
British Transport Docks Board	21.0	15.0	14.1	9.4	10.3	6.8	9.6	12.2	10	11
British Waterways Board	1.0	1.1	1.2	1.7	1.0	1.2	1.4	1.4	1	–
Transport Holding Company	0.3	0.7	0.7	0.4	–	–	–	–	–	–
National Freight Corporation	38.9	33.5	19.7	14.9	26.2	21.0	32.0	33.0	34	35
National Bus Company	16.4	17.9	18.3	17.3	24.9	14.3	23.7	23.7	24	24
Scottish Transport Group	4.9	4.2	3.4	6.7	6.5	5.9	5.5	5.5	6	6
Total surface transport industries	214.4	206.0	169.0	181.5	211.7	192.4	269.6	308.5	322	324
Grand total	1566.4	1702.8	1617.5	1628.6	1808.5	1957.1	2120.6	2146.3	2177	2206

Index

THE URBAN AND REGIONAL PLANNING SERIES

Other Books in the Series

CHADWICK, G. F.
A Systems View of Planning: Towards a Theory of the Urban and Regional Planning Process (Volume 1)

BLUNDEN, W. R.
The Land Use/Transport System: Analysis and Synthesis (Volume 2)

GOODALL, B.
The Economics of Urban Areas (Volume 3)

LEE, C.
Models in Planning: An Introduction to the Use of Quantitative Models in Planning (Volume 4)

FALUDI, A.
A Reader in Planning Theory (Volume 5)

COWLING, T. M. and STEELEY, G. C.
Sub-Regional Planning Studies: An Evaluation (Volume 6)

FALUDI, A.
Planning Theory (Volume 7)

SOLESBURY, W.
Policy in Urban Planning: Structure plans, programmes and local plans (Volume 8)

MOSELEY, M. J.
Growth Centres in Spatial Planning (Volume 9)

LICHFIELD, N., *et al.*
Evaluation in the Planning Process (Volume 10)

SANT, M. E. C.
Industrial Movement and Regional Development: The British Case (Volume 11)

HART, D.
Strategic Planning in London: The Rise and Fall of the Primary Road Network (Volume 12)

Other Titles of Interest

CLOUT, H. D.
Rural Geography

JOHNSON, J. H.
Urban Geography, 2nd Edition

The terms of our inspection copy service apply to all the above books. A complete catalogue of all books in the Pergamon International Library is available on request. The Publisher will be pleased to consider suggestions for revised editions and new titles.